Golden Years
of
Poole

Part of the
Memories
series

*The Publishers would like to thank the following companies for supporting
the production of this book*

Dolphin Shopping Centre

The Dorset Glass Company Limited

J A Hawkes & Son Limited

James & Son

The Ryvita Company Limited

Sunseeker International (Boats) Limited

First published in Great Britain by True North Books Limited
Units 3 - 5 Heathfield Industrial Park
Elland West Yorkshire
HX5 9AE
Tel. 01422 377977
© Copyright: True North Books Limited 1999

ISBN 1 900463 69 5

Text, design and origination by True North Books Limited
Printed and bound by The Amadeus Press Limited

Memories are made of this

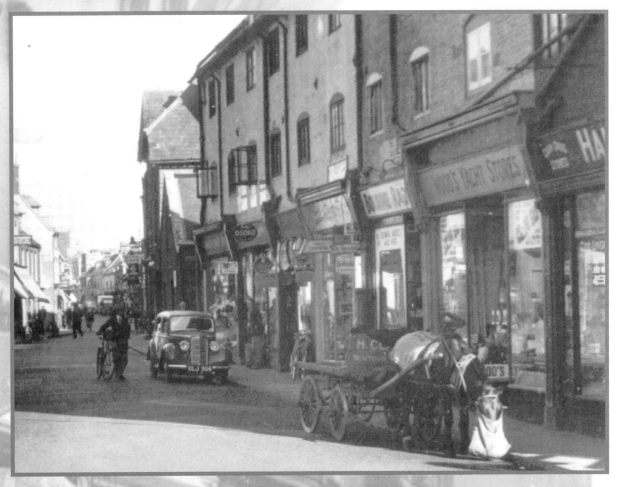

Memories. We all have them: people, places and events, some good and some bad. Our memories of the place where we grew up are usually tucked away in a very special place in our mind. The best are probably connected with our childhood and youth, when we longed to be grown up and paid no attention to adults who told us to enjoy being young, as these were the best years of our lives. We look back now and realise that they were right.

Old photographs bring our memories flooding back - coronations and celebrations; talking pictures, Technicolour and television; the war years, rationing, and the shared hopes and fears which created such a warm community spirit; buying things made of nylon and plastic; fashions which took trouserbottoms and hemlines from drainpipes and mini-skirts to the other extreme; Doris Day, Acker Bilk, Elvis Presley and the Beatles; the jitterbug, the tango and discos; Ford Populars and Minis; decimalisation. Life changed so much over the years. Some changes were big, some small; some altered our lives in ways we never anticipated. Who in the early days of motoring could have foreseen the motorways and traffic systems of the latter decades of the 20th century? Did any of us realise, when we first saw a computer, what a tremendous impact they would have on our lives? Self-service supermarkets and frozen food made our lives easier - but at the expense of our friendly little corner shops. Nostalgia is always such a mixture of feelings . . . We hope that the collection of pictures in this book will remind you of happy days in bygone eras - and who knows, you might even have been there when one of the photographs was taken!

Contents

Poole through the years

Nothing ever stays the same. Many would agree that as far as the town they grew up in is concerned, they could wish that it had, while others have welcomed the redevelopments which so drastically changed the face of Poole. But from its establishment as a significant harbour towards the end of the 14th century, the town has never stood still.

It was the trading links with Newfoundland which brought wealth to the town and led to the construction of many of its fine Georgian buildings, and though the trade came to an end in the 19th century, the expansion of nearby Bournemouth had a 'knock on' effect, and firms grew up in Poole specialising in importing timber, roofing materials and other building materials. But it was the local clay which was to form the basis of Poole's most significant industry, and by 1855 around 40,000 tons of clay was leaving Poole for Merseyside every year, en route to the Staffordshire potteries.

Poole has had a picturesque past. Deaths from bubonic plague and the building of pest houses, evading the notorious press gang, pirates, ghosts and public whippings - all these ingredients from a bygone age have gone into the town's melting pot. In more recent times, Poole played an important part in many second world war operations, from the Dunkirk evacuation to the D-Day landings.

We are fortunate that the 20th century was so well chronicled, and this collection of fascinating images call to mind the town and its inhabitants 50, 60 and even 70 years ago. Poole carnival, boat racing, beating the bounds, boy scouts and girl guides, Branksome Chine and open air dancing - all find their way into the pages of this book.

We hope that you will read and enjoy 'Golden Years of Poole' - and remember that history is still in the making.

At leisure

Below: Sunshine and blue skies was a vital ingredient to a day spent outdoors, though for those less than perfect days the Solarium presented sun worshippers with an alternative way to acquire that continental bronzed look. The first facility of its kind to be opened in Britain, the Solarium was built by Poole Council in 1932. It offered 'electric beams of the artificial sun' - namely ultra-violet lamps - where even on overcast or chilly days clients of all ages could don their bathing costumes and, unaware of the danger, work on their tan. The ultra-violet rays, advertised as 'health giving', were in fact very powerful and while they could indeed aid the formation of vitamin D in the skin, they could at the same time cause sunburn with its associated side-effects. A town guide from the 1930s tells us that the Solarium had its own 'vita-glass tea lounge' (what?), and that in winter 'one may enjoy within its walls artificial sunshine and summer heat'. More energetic visitors, however, preferred to walk its natural woodland paths among the Douglas firs and Monterey pines and, in June, the brilliantly coloured rhododendrons, and wonder at the breath-taking views of the chine's natural beauty.

Branksome Chine has long been a favourite beauty spot, for local people as well as for the many visitors to the town, and though the heavy clouds of war were hanging over the country when these views were captured, no shadow of gloom hangs over the happy scene.

The tasteful continental cafe, with its sun terrace lined with little tables under brightly coloured parasols, was the perfect place to take afternoon tea and cream cakes after a dip in the sea or a couple of hours spent relaxing in a deckchair.

Events of the 1930s

HOT OFF THE PRESS

The years of the 1930s saw Adolf Hitler's sickening anti-Jewish campaign echoed in the streets of Britain. On 19th October 1936 Oswald Mosley's 7,000-strong British Union of Fascists clashed head on with thousands of Jews and Communists in London, resulting in 80 people being injured in the ensuing battle. Mosley and his 'blackshirts' later rampaged through the streets beating up Jews and smashing the windows of their businesses.

GETTING AROUND

At the beginning of the decade many believed that the airship was the transport of the future. The R101 airship, however, loaded with thousands of cubic metres of hydrogen, crashed in France on its maiden flight in 1930. Forty-eight passengers and crew lost their lives. In 1937 the Hindenburg burst into flames - the entire disaster caught on camera and described by a distraught reporter. The days of the airship were numbered.

SPORTING CHANCE

In 1939 British racing driver Sir Malcolm Campbell hit the headlines when he captured the world's water-speed record for the third time in 'Bluebird' - all his cars were given the same name. A racing driver who set world speed records both on land and on water, Sir Malcolm established world land-speed records no fewer than nine times. His son Donald went on to set further records, tragically dying in 1967 when his speedboat - also named 'Bluebird' - crashed.

If the weather outside was a little too chilly, the swimming pool at Sandbanks Hotel offered bathers an alternative which they might have described as 'absolutely spiffing' . These swimmers, both ladies and gents, were having a lot of fun when they were snapped by a photographer. The hotel had provided a great variety of equipment: while one young lady is thinking of doing a

bit of rope climbing (will she make it, from her position in the water?), another sits on a swing over the pool. Why don't we have this kind of equipment today? Think what fun those swings would be! Watched by a very tall man - perhaps a member of staff? - another young lady is about to make a splash via the chute. The management have placed little tables around the edge of the pool, where visitors and friends can sit and watch the fun, and perhaps have a tray of tea brought through. Or, as the Sandbanks Hotel was fully licensed, they might prefer something a little stronger.

Left: This was The Gladiators, 1940s style, and the rules of the game seemed simple enough, being to knock your opponent off the pole and into the drink. This contest, however, had a further drawback that would seem most unfair - though it was one which was calculated to give the crowd a good laugh. Let them try it themselves if they could do better, might have been the challenge from the contestants, as the pole bridging the ship to shore gap was greased. Trying to keep your balance on a greasy pole while dodging your opponent's sandbag and at the same time swinging your own bag to dislodge him was a feat that resembled chasing a greased pig through the sand dunes while riding a monocycle. Cheered on by a huge crowd of mainly male spectators, this particular 'Wolf' has succeeded in unseating the other guy and giving him an unwanted bath. But how long will he keep his own seat, we wonder? What a pity that we do not know what this occasion was. Perhaps a more mature reader will recognise himself among the crowd - or as the victorious competitor!

Above: The miniature railway in Poole Park - which even had its own station - was a hugely popular attraction, and was probably described by its passengers as 'super-duper'; today of course it would be 'cool' or even 'wicked', especially if you were lucky enough to be the driver. Driving the little steam engine would have been a much-envied position, and there were many railway enthusiasts who would have been glad to part with cash from their own pockets for the privilege of driving this little beauty around the park. However it was described, the little train was still reckoned to be great fun, and a ride was all part of a day out in Poole Park. The park has long had many attractions especially for children, from its aviaries of colourful birds to its model yacht pond, and in 1963 a children's zoo of 120 animals and birds was opened. All very thrilling stuff, and calculated to send any child home tired and satisfied at the end of a wonderful day out.

Feeling hot? The paddling pool at Sandbanks Pavilion is an ideal place to cool off - if you are six years old, that is! Kiddies in sun hats and swim suits (remember how itchy those woollen ones were?) splash around in the water; one has his bucket with him; is it about to be emptied over the head of his sister, we wonder? A boy nearby would obviously like a rubber ring of his own, but he is improvising, as children did in those non-materialistic days, with a car inner tube. Just as effective, and big enough for two! With Brownsea Island in the background, this view over the car park - far smaller then than now - will evoke many childhood memories among our readers. This 1930s scene

reveals a car park which is rapidly filling up; note the covers which many drivers have used to protect the paintwork of their precious cars from the glare of the sun. Not too many years hence, however, the second world war would bring petrol rationing and a chronic shortage of spare parts, and many of these cars would be garaged for the duration of the war.

Events of the 1930s

SCIENCE AND DISCOVERY
By observing the heavens, astronomers had long believed that there in the constellation of Gemini lay a new planet, so far undiscovered. They began to search for the elusive planet, and a special astronomical camera was built for the purpose. The planet Pluto was discovered by amateur astronomer Clyde Tombaugh in 1930, less than a year later.

WHAT'S ON?
In this heyday of the cinema, horrified audiences were left gasping at the sight of Fay Wray in the clutches of the giant ape in the film 'King Kong', released in 1933. Very different but just as gripping was the gutsy 1939 American Civil War romance 'Gone with the Wind'. Gable's parting words, 'Frankly, my dear, I don't give a damn' went down in history.

ROYAL WATCH
The talking point of the early 1930s was the affair of the Prince of Wales, who later became King Edward VIII, and American divorcee Wallis Simpson. Faced with a choice, Edward gave up his throne for 'the woman I love' and spent the remainder of his life in exile. Many supported him, though they might not have been as keen to do so if they had been aware of his Nazi sympathies, kept strictly under wraps at the time.

This page: In spite of the darkness, flags fly atop the poles, and rows of deck chairs arrayed around the edge of the outdoor dance floor at Sandbanks Pavilion offer dancers an opportunity to rest their aching feet *(above)*. Wouldn't it be nice to know what occasion this was? We can be reasonably certain, given the number of bare arms and strappy sandals among the ladies, that it was not a New Year or Christmas ball! The fascinating photograph probably dates from the 1930s, yet some reader with a long memory will surely remember whether outdoor dancing was a regular event at the Pavilion. This was obviously a very jolly occasion, and whether you were nine years old and dancing with your father, or had to make do with your girl friend or even, horror of horrors, your kid brother, you were out on the dance floor and doing the barn dance with the rest. The band, smart in their caps and uniforms, were fortunate in finding a still night - there is no breath of light breeze to blow the music off their stands! Those were the days when the Veleta, the Military Two-Step and the Gay Gordons would have been danced; had the Lancers come in at the time? Sandbanks Pavilion had a very different atmosphere during the day *(above right)*. A pleasant summer's day has tempted different groups of people out in this shot from the late 1930s or perhaps 40s, some to work on their tan while they read a good book, others to take their deck chairs into the shade. Note the chair in the right foreground; when did you last see a chair with its own built-in sunshade?

This page: The names Harvey and Davis will be familiar to many of our readers, who will remember their ferry services between Sandbanks and Studland. The two firms ran a rival service, though we can see from their identical price of 3d for the crossing - a bargain at the price - that they were not involved in a price war *(above)!* This is a happy scene of summer holiday fun, and a young family make their way towards the shore; have they decided to travel on the 'floating bridge' - or will they opt for Harveys, nearby? Dad leads the way, while Mum follows on behind with the essential rubber ring tucked under her arm. The kiddies, dressed appropriately in their swimming costumes (and a sun hat), have their spades at the ready, and are full of excitement at the prospect of a day on the beach. The man wearing plus-fours is perhaps the owner of the bicycle parked near the tolls cabin.

This fascinating view was captured before the pier was blown up in the second world war. The war sadly put paid to two craft belonging to the rival firms; Tom Davis's 'Island Queen' and Harvey's 'Southern Queen' were both destroyed during the Dunkirk evacuation in 1940, though one of the Harvey brothers' craft, the 'Ferry Nymph', came through the experience unscathed and afterwards carried a brass plate to commemorate her involvement at Dunkirk.

The 'Ferry Sprite' in the foreground *(below)* is almost empty of passengers, while her sister ship, the 'Ferry Naiad', appears to be about to moor at the jetty to allow a boat-load of day trippers to disembark for an afternoon of fun in the sun at Sandbanks.

Left: *The photographer recorded a tense moment during Poole Regatta (the year unfortunately unknown) as, encouraged by a few young fans and helpers, the crews embarked for their race. Which of these enthusiastic crews actually won that year, we wonder? The town had its regatta as early as the mid nineteenth century, and even at that time the rowing event was part and parcel of the occasion. Sailing boats of all kinds took part, each in their own class, from 15-foot sailing boats to yachts of up to 25 tons - and all decorated with brightly coloured bunting and flags. The first prize of £20 would have represented a sizeable amount of cash back then - more than enough for each member of the crew to enjoy a decent night out and still have some left over! Many of Poole's events, naturally enough, centre around boats and water (among them Youth Afloat, the Powerboat Race and the Fishermen's Regatta) and today's regatta, usually held in June, is now held in Poole Park.*

Below: *The cars are in the Haven Hotel car park, the spectators have found themselves a good viewpoint, and the faces - most of them - are turned towards the sea. But what are these people looking at? We can only guess that this was the occasion of one of the many boat races which have long been a big draw during the summer season. The main action, however, has obviously yet to start as at least one lady in the crowd has settled down in her deck chair (far more comfortable than the steps) to catch up on the day's news. The photograph appears to have been taken at lunch time, as the gentleman shading his eyes, and his wife, have brought sandwiches with them to stave off the pangs of hunger (or are they indulging in an ice cream?). Others who were less far sighted could, of course, take luncheon or afternoon tea in the Haven Hotel. The photograph is unfortunately undated, though as few of the men are wearing hats - the prevailing fashion before the 1950s - we could take a rough guess at that decade.*

Around the town centre

Traffic was free to use the High Street at the time of the photograph, yet this tranquil scene captured one sunny day early in the 20th century only reveals a few handcarts and a cycle or two. Shady hats and ankle-length hemlines are much in evidence among the Edwardian ladies, who would have been very shocked if they could have taken a glimpse into the future to view the costume worn by women at the beginning of the 21st century! A sharp eye might spot the clock above Coles Jewellers in the distance; a little nearer to us is the Bulls Head, a very old coaching inn, better known to us today as the premises of the Poole Herald. Nearby was the firm of Sharp and Son, whose sign was a huge key. Sharps were ironmongers as well as locksmiths. Bacon and Curtis the gardening and hardware shop in the left foreground is taking advantage of the dry weather to display a wheelbarrow, gardening tools and watering cans. Those were the days well before James Dyson's innovative ballbarrows - in fact gardening in general involved more hard work all round. Lawn mowers owned by the average family would have been of the push-pull persuasion, unaided by petrol or electricity and depending on muscle power alone. Long live the Flymo....

Events of the 1930s

MELODY MAKERS

Throughout the 1930s a young American trombonist called Glenn Miller was making his mark in the world of music. By 1939 the Glenn Miller sound was a clear leader in the field; his clean-cut, meticulously executed arrangements of numbers such as 'A String of Pearls' and 'Moonlight Serenade' brought him fame across the world as a big-band leader. During a flight to England from Paris in 1944 Miller's plane disappeared; no wreckage was ever found.

THE WORLD AT LARGE

In India, Gandhi's peaceful protests against British rule were gathering momentum. The Salt Laws were a great bone of contention: forced to buy salt from the British government, thousands of protestors marched to the salt works, intending to take it over in the name of the Indian people. Policemen and guards attacked the marchers, but not one of them fought back. Gandhi, who earned for himself the name 'Mahatma' - Great Soul - was assassinated in 1948.

INVENTION AND TECHNOLOGY

With no driving tests or speed restrictions, 120,000 people were killed on the roads in Britain between the two world wars. In 1934 Percy Shaw, invented a safety device destined to become familiar the world over: reflecting roadstuds. In dark or foggy conditions the studs that reflected light from the car's headlights kept traffic on the 'straight and narrow' and must over the years have saved many lives.

Pedestrians outnumber the vehicles in this early view of the High Street in this early view that perhaps dates from the 1930s or even earlier. Those were the days when many families were feeling the pinch, and Tusans, the pawnbroker on the left, would have seen a brisk trade. At the time, men had more inhibitions about being seen pushing prams or carrying flowers, yet the man outside the Home and Colonial has braved the raised eyebrows and is taking a bunch home for his wife.

In the first half of the 20th century there were many small grocers, butchers and bakers in the High Street. Small grocery chains such as the Home and Colonial were the traditional way to shop, and customers would queue to be served while the assistant weighed out butter from a huge slab and sliced bacon while you waited - a far cry from today's plastic packs! Things were to remain that way until the mid-1950s, when self-service shopping began to catch on. Supermarkets came to Poole town centre - then departed again when out of town shopping came to stay. The Bulls Head on the right - later to become the offices of the Poole Advertiser - was still open at the time of the photograph. It was during alterations to the offices that a beautiful moulded ceiling dating from around 1600 was found.

Bunting flies high in front of the old Almshouses and along Church Street and Market Street, but without knowing the date of the photograph we can not pinpoint the occasion. It could have been King George VI's coronation in May 1937, the VE-day celebrations, or even our Queen's coronation in 1953. We will never know....

How many buildings built during the reign of Henry V are still occupied today? At least one, we can answer, as St George's Almshouses were still in use at the beginning of the 21st! Many alterations have of course been made to the ancient building; new chimney stacks were erected, probably in the 17th century, and major restoration took place in 1904. The houses were, in estate agents' parlance, 'compact', having just two tiny rooms and a pantry, and at one time an upper floor was added to the tiny homes - which was for some reason later abandoned. The houses, originally built for the four priests who served the four altars at St James' church, were for the next 500 years occupied by the poor of the parish.

Above: Cars are making their presence felt in this pre-war photograph of Poole High Street, with not a double-yellow line in sight! Traffic levels were set to increase, however: between 1953 and 1963 the number of cars in the country had risen from one car for every twenty-four people to one for every seven. Pedestrianisation of the High Street brought relief to the old town centre, and shoppers could once more relax and browse in safety. Interestingly, Woolworths was still designated as '3d and 6d Stores' at the time of the photograph. This was a direct echo of the original '5 and 10 cent Stores' that spread in a chain across America at the end of the 19th Century. Two doors along, Burtons had established a firm presence in the town. Montague Burton's good quality menswear has been a firm favourite with gentlemen for many years, and virtually every town and city in Britain has at least one branch. The story goes that when soldiers were demobbed after military service they were given vouchers to be outfitted at Burtons. They went along to the nearest branch and were kitted out in what was termed 'the full Monty' - a phrase which has in recent years come to mean something very different from a full suit of clothes!

Top: Like Big Brother, a rather unnerving pair of eyes gazes down on the left from opticians Perry & Co, keeping tabs on the passers-by in the High Street. This scene is made all the more fascinating by the amount of detail which is revealed by close inspection. Near the opticians, three children are hurrying to cross the road; the Green Cross Code was yet to be, but fortunately the kiddies are in no danger from passing traffic. Still on the left, Burtons menswear - a firm favourite with gentlemen for many years - are holding a sale. The London Hotel, whose prominent sign advertises 'Grill and Garage', was built in the 18th century. The hotel was badly damaged in World War II bombing raids and was rebuilt around 1950. It was renamed The Old Harry in 1960.

What an amazing range of goods and services was available in the High Street at the time of the photograph! You could pop in and have a haircut or a shave, buy Kodak film at Arnotts, get your prescription filled (or perhaps buy a home remedy) at Timothy White's, browse among the engagement and wedding rings at Cole's, fit yourself up with a pair of shoes and your dog with his dinner before sitting down to enjoy a 'pure cream ice'. Marvellous.

Below: Refuelling your vehicle once involved attaching a nosebag rather than a diesel nozzle... In a scene of pure nostalgia we can recapture the real atmosphere of the old town centre, and the way things used to be. Pedestrianisation was unknown and unneeded at the time; the 1930s were still the days when noise from the town's traffic involved the rattle of wheels and the trotting of hooves, and any 'traffic pollution' could be put to good use on your floribundas. Two of the town's historic pubs stand side by side on the left of the photograph - the King's Head (serving Hall & Woodhouse's Blandford Ales which were 'drawn from the wood'), and the Antelope. Apparently, the King's Head - at one time the Plume of Feathers - was the favoured watering-hole of the sea captains of old, who literally made their mark on the establishment by signing their names on the glass panelled door. The Antelope was first built as far back as the 16th century, was remodelled in the 18th, and was given an extra storey in the 19th. Note the antelope and the flagpole mounted above the door at third floor level.

Right: The old and the new side by side - though it would take a keen eye to spot the old horse-drawn cart making its way down the High Street alongside a motor car. The days of the horse and cart, however, were numbered and the car was about to reign supreme - though those days were far in the future on the day this photograph was taken. How many readers remember quenching their thirst at the London Hotel, on the right? Remember the fascinating mural featuring old Poole characters which was painted around the walls of the lounge? The painting, done in 1936, was the work of C Todd, with the help of students from Poole Art School. In 1960 the Bass brewery renamed the pub the Old Harry after a notorious Poole pirate. Across the road Hawkes Shoes, on the extreme left of the photograph, is today run by Andrew Hawkes, great-great-grandson of Joseph Charles Hawkes, who founded the family firm back in 1847. Wouldn't it be interesting to take a peep into the windows of Timothy Whites, next door - who, judging by the baskets hanging outside, were obviously much more than a chemist's shop at the time.

Bottom: As we can see by the memorable vehicles in the shot, this was Kingland Crescent in the 1960s, before the old bus terminus, which then lay just off to the left, was moved to the other side of the Dolphin Centre. Still there, and still going places, this same crescent of busy shops today has no fewer than four travel agents, all competing to take you for a safari in Kenya or a winter holiday in Cyprus.

The rather unfamiliar yet gleaming and well cared-for car in the foreground has been identified as a Hillman Minx California. Instantly recognisable, however, is the little white Mini behind, voted the car of the century in 1999 as it celebrated its 40th birthday. The Mini - practical, affordable and fuel-efficient - was introduced to British drivers in 1959 by Alexander Issigonis, who was knighted in 1969 for his contribution to British design, and by the time he died in 1988 more than five million Minis had been sold. Beyond the Mini is a Ford Zephyr (or possibly a Zodiac), while the Ford Anglia further back will evoke fond memories among those readers who learned to drive in one.

Right: The Dolphin Hotel - a familiar name to most of our readers, who will remember its rather nice restaurant. When the hotel was built in 1903 in Towngate Street it was The Longfleet, only later becoming the Dolphin. In a further name change it was to eventually become the Jolly Miller,

a lively disco pub which attracted a host of younger punters. Plans to demolish the building in the late 1980s met with a storm of protest, and supporters campaigned vigorously to save it. The planners' red pen prevailed, however, and a parade of shops in Falklands Square stand today on the site of the old Dolphin Hotel.

Some memorable vehicles stand along the kerbside, though they are difficult to identify accurately. The car in the left foreground is surely an old Ford Anglia, while the owners of what could be a Ford Thames van and a Standard Vanguard have perhaps decided to lunch at the Dolphin restaurant. Rather prone to rust, the Vanguard's American styling and well-sprung ride nevertheless made it attractive to many. Sadly, this was not a car to withstand the test of time, and few survive today.

Events & occasions

This page and overleaf: It's carnival time in Poole, and a large group of pretty fisher girls in colourful costumes portray Poole's fishing industry, which dates back hundreds of years *(above)*. Its oyster beds were world famous even in the 17th century, when Poole oysters, praised by the writer Daniel Defoe, were pickled for export. The carnival gave those entering their floats a real opportunity to illustrate the town's rich history, so much of it centred around the sea and ships. These young ladies, carrying their baskets and bearing long-handled nets, appear to be very sure of their seats on the flat cart and are looking forward to an afternoon of fun. The horse, however, which was clearly expected to draw all 13 of them and the cart as well, might not have been having such a good time....

Events of the 1940s

WHAT'S ON?

In wartime Britain few families were without a wireless set. It was the most popular form of entertainment, and programmes such as ITMA, Music While You Work and Workers' Playtime provided the people with an escape from the harsh realities of bombing raids and ration books. In 1946 the BBC introduced the Light Programme, the Home Service and the Third Programme, which gave audiences a wider choice of listening.

GETTING AROUND

October 1948 saw the production of Britain's first new car designs since before the war. The Morris Minor was destined for fame as one of the most popular family cars, while the four-wheel-drive Land Rover answered the need for a British-made off-road vehicle. The country was deeply in the red, however, because of overseas debts incurred during the war. The post-war export drive that followed meant that British drivers had a long wait for their own new car.

SPORTING CHANCE

American World Heavyweight Boxing Champion Joe Louis, who first took the title back in 1937, ruled the world of boxing during the 1930s and 40s, making a name for himself as unbeatable. Time after time he successfully defended his title against all comers, finally retiring in 1948 after fighting an amazing 25 title bouts throughout his boxing career. Louis died in 1981 at the age of 67.

These striking photographs are certainly pre-war, though we cannot pinpoint the actual year. The tradition of Poole Carnival was established in 1913, and the carnival secretary Bert Cutler made a name for himself as the man who unerringly picked a sunny day for the event. The carnival was naturally discontinued during the second world war, and there was yet another glitch between 1978 and 1983, when a disagreement between two charity groups put the event on hold.

The carnival developed from an original sports meet arranged by Poole shop assistants. Perhaps this float with a 'Wild West' flavour - eagerly watched from upstairs windows - dates from that era *(inset)*? The staff of Hawkes shoes in the High Street

were the native Americans in splendid costume, complete with a well-constructed Indian teepee - and the reason that particular theme was chosen was to advertised the store's range of moccasins. Is the leather draped behind the driver a sample of the material actually used to manufacture the moccasins, we wonder? It's unfortunate that the names of these staff members is unknown to us; we can see that two of these young 'Indians' are very young, perhaps school leavers. We must bear in mind, of course, that the school leaving age was only raised to 15 with the 1944 Education Act.

Even the horse is bedecked in ribbons and rosettes for the Poole carnival, the rosette between her ears making her look especially fetching *(main picture)*. At least 12 young clowns are aboard the cart, though we cannot be certain as their two-tone face make-up acts as very good camouflage! Local charities such as the Cornelia Hospital benefited from the proceeds of the carnival, and the event became hugely popular in the town. Dense crowds of spectators would line the procession route to watch the long parade of imaginatively decorated floats pass by.

Both pages: His Royal Highness the Prince of Wales - later King Edward VII - visited Poole in 1890 to declare open the new Poole Park. The gentleman in the carriage, courteously raising his hat to the ladies, would appear to be the Prince *(facing page, top)*. Looks, however, can deceive, and the 'Prince of Wales' is actually a resident of Poole, very adequately acting the part in the Poole Pageant. The Pageant, staged in Poole Park between 4th and 16th August 1952, was a breathtaking event.

February of that year saw our Queen's accession to the throne, and the Pageant, which celebrated Poole's long history, was a fitting way for the entire town to celebrate the occasion. Throughout the twelve days of the Pageant, different 'chapters' told the story of Poole's development and growth across more than 1800 years, from AD44 to the visit of the Prince of Wales in 1890. The Roman occupation of Hamworthy and the attack made by Danes, was acted out in Chapter 1, followed by the granting of the town's first Charter by William Longespee in 1249 (which cost 70 marks, around £4,000 today) The granting of the Charter was an important date in Poole's history. Longespee, one of the warlike earls of Salisbury, was unusually tall, and he actually took his name from his long sword. History tells us that he used the money to go on a crusade, though he might have lived longer if he'd stayed at home - he met a violent death there in 1249. Could the granting of the Charter be the scene being acted out in the photograph on the facing page?

The visit of King Charles II in 1665, the Battle of Quiberon Bay, and the activities of the notorious press gang all added their own flavour to the

occasion, bringing history to life. The Masque of Neptune *(below)* told the story of Harry Paye, the well known Poole pirate, who returned from his buccaneering with a shipload of treasure and jewels.

On the very last day of the Pageant 'Princess Alexandra', as regal as in real life, and 'Lady Wimborne' both received bouquets of flowers for playing their parts so well, and the marvellous event ended with 'God Bless the Prince of Wales', played by the Poole Town Band.

It's 'eyes right' for the line of Girl Guides outside the Municipal Buildings as the Mayoral procession emerges. Full regalia was the order of the day, and in the foreground Miss Margaret Llewellin, who at the time was the Sheriff of Poole (later to become the town's first woman Mayor), is resplendent in her chain of office and ceremonial fur-trimmed cape. It is thought that the bowler-hatted gentleman by her side is Lord Shaftesbury, the Lord Lieutenant of Dorset. In the background, mace bearers, proudly wearing their medals, walk ahead of the Mayor - though there is no sign here of the real celebrity of the day, the

Chief Guide, Lady Olave Baden-Powell. During her visit to Poole Lady Baden-Powell was taken to the site of the very first Scout camp on Brownsea Island - though it was unlikely that the original Union Jack that flew over the camp would have been raised in her honour; that particular flag, riddled with bullet holes, had flown at Mafeking.

Events of the 1940s

HOT OFF THE PRESS
At the end of World War II in 1945 the Allies had their first sight of the unspeakable horrors of the Nazi extermination camps they had only heard of until then. In January, 4,000 emaciated prisoners more dead than alive were liberated by the Russians from Auschwitz in Poland, where three million people, most of them Jews, were murdered. The following year 23 prominent Nazis faced justice at Nuremberg; 12 of them were sentenced to death for crimes against humanity.

THE WORLD AT LARGE
The desert area of Alamogordo in New Mexico was the scene of the first atomic bomb detonation on July 16, 1945. With an explosive power equal to more than 15,000 tons of TNT, the flash could be seen 180 miles away. President Truman judged that the bomb could secure victory over Japan with far less loss of US lives than a conventional invasion, and on 6th August the first of the new weapons was dropped on Hiroshima. Around 80,000 people died.

ROYAL WATCH
By the end of World War II, the 19-year-old Princess Elizabeth and her distant cousin Lieutenant Philip Mountbatten RN were already in love. The King and Queen approved of Elizabeth's choice of husband, though they realised that she was rather young and had not mixed with many other young men. The engagement announcement was postponed until the Princess had spent four months on tour in Africa. The couple's wedding on 20th November 1947 was a glittering occasion - the first royal pageantry since before the war.

Both pages: It was a big day for Poole when the Chief Guide, Lady Baden-Powell, was presented with the Freedom of the Borough - made even more special by the fact that her husband, Lt Col Sir Robert Baden-Powell, had also received the Freedom of the Borough in 1929. The date was 20th May 1950, and the girl guides and boy scouts were out in full force to give a warm welcome to the wife of the founder of the scouting movement *(below)*. The movement was formed in 1908, following the publication of Sir Robert Baden-Powell's book 'Scouting for Boys'. The book had been intended for use by existing youth organisations, but it proved to be the beginning of a new one. Baden-Powell's ideas on the training of young boys differed from others, as he included such activities as signalling, rope-knotting, mapping, first aid and other skills needed in camping and similar outdoor activities which developed self-reliance. The movement became popular and quickly spread from Britain to other countries - and a similar movement was set up, of course, for girls. During her visit the Chief Guide, accompanied by Miss Margaret Llewellin, the Sheriff of Poole, inspected the Guides and Scouts, who lined up smartly for her, proudly wearing the uniform of the movement *(right)*. Also thrilled to meet the lady during her visit to the town were two original members of Lord Baden-Powell's first camp, set up on Brownsea Island in 1907. The year after this memorable event, Lord Baden-Powell died.

This page: It was a fine sunny day when the Sea Scouts paraded proudly under their flags on the Quay, watched, it would seem, by a number of parents; a few mothers wearing the typical cloche hats of the period can be detected behind the back rows *(below right)*. As far as we can judge, the photograph dates from the 1930s - years which were less than affluent for many families. The boys have obviously dressed as smartly as they could under their differing circumstances, though their footwear ranges from shoes and pumps to sandals and wellington boots! Many of these lads had obviously worked hard to acquire various skills to gain the badges and medals we can see on their chests and sleeves. The premises of J R Wood and Co Ltd, advertising themselves as 'factors, shippers and merchants' can be seen in the background. Was it on the same day, we wonder, that this second picture of the scouts was taken as they walked past the Customs House *(right)?* The parade must surely by this time have disbanded, as a couple of the older Sea Scouts, unaware that future generations would frown on their habit, can wait no longer and have lit up their cigarettes.

The Sea Scouts were a popular and prestigious organisation which we can best describe as Boy Scouts with a nautical flavour! The Sea Cadets, formed in 1938, were a similar but separate organisation which had a flourishing unit in Poole. During the second world war the unit became 150-strong. Apparently many of the young men joined the Navy after training with the Sea Cadets. Instruction in sailing, sports, navigation, shooting, boatwork and even band tuition formed part of their training, and in 1981 an efficiency burgee, the highest achievement the Admiralty can bestow, was presented to the Poole Sea Cadets.

Readers who were scouts or guides will remember the influence it had on their lives

How many readers will recognise themselves as one of these cub scouts, photographed back in 1950? The occasion was the presentation of the Freedom of the Borough to Lady Baden-Powell, and these lads will have been well primed beforehand as to the importance of the lady's connection with the scouting movement. The photograph captures Lady Baden-Powell at the microphone, and it would be fascinating to know what she was saying to these youngsters - though it's more than likely the subject of her talk that day quickly escaped their memory.

Be that as it may, the majority of the boys appear to be listening intently to the Chief Guide's every word. From the very beginning of the scouting movement in the early years of the 20th century leaders placed great emphasis on personal integrity, and before they were accepted as a scout each of these young boys would have had to promise to do their duty to God and to their country, to help other people, and to obey the Scout law. Readers who were scouts or guides in their youth will remember just how great an influence the movement had on their lives.

Events of the 1940s

MELODY MAKERS

The songs of radio personalities such as Bing Crosby and Vera Lynn were whistled, sung and hummed everywhere during the 1940s. The 'forces' sweetheart' brought hope to war-torn Britain with 'When the Lights go on Again', while the popular crooner's 'White Christmas' is still played around Christmas time even today. Who can forget songs like 'People Will Say we're in Love', 'Don't Fence Me In', 'Zip-a-dee-doo-dah', and 'Riders in the Sky'?

INVENTION AND TECHNOLOGY

Inspired by quick-drying printers' ink, in 1945 Hungarian journalist Laszlo Biro developed a ballpoint pen which released viscous ink from its own reservoir as the writer moved the pen across the page. An American inventor was working on a similar idea at the same time, but it was Biro's name that stuck. A few years later Baron Bich developed a low cost version of the pen, and the 'Bic' ballpoint went on sale in France in 1953.

SCIENCE AND DISCOVERY

In 1943 Ukrainian-born biochemist Selman Abraham Waksman made a significant discovery. While studying organisms found in soil he discovered an antibiotic (a name Waksman himself coined) which was later found to be the very first effective treatment for tuberculosis. A major killer for thousands of years, even the writings of the ancient Egyptians contain stories of people suffering from tuberculosis. Waksman's development of streptomycin brought him the 1952 Nobel Prize for Medicine.

It's 1964, and hundreds of people have congregated in front of the Customs House to watch the ceremony of 'Beating the Bounds' - and join in the fun when the usual band of 'pirates' decide to play their own unscheduled part in the proceedings *(inset)*. The 12-man jury, dressed in the appropriate naval costume, appears to be in the process of being sworn in before setting sail around the boundaries of the three-mile stretch of water which came under the jurisdiction of the Mayor as Admiral of the port. The ancient ceremony was established back in 1364, when the Winchelsea Certificate was granted to the town of Poole, confirming the Admiral's authority.

The proceedings traditionally started off on the steps of the historic Customs House, which was built in 1813 to replace an 18th century Customs House, destroyed by fire that same year. The new building was an exact replica of the earlier Customs House - which was itself an exact copy of the Red Lion Coffee House which preceded it. On the extreme left of the photograph is the Town Cellars, or Woolhouse, a medieval warehouse where wool and cloth for export was stored - today the Maritime Museum. An air of suppressed excitement hangs over the huge crowd on the quay in the photograph from a much earlier year *(main picture)*. Though there is not a Jolly Roger in sight, the atmosphere of the scene leads us to believe that this could also be the 'Beating of the Bounds' - unless, of course, you know better? The photograph probably dates from the 1930s; the ceremony, which had been discontinued in 1835 when the law was changed and Poole Corporation no longer had the jurisdiction of the harbour, was revived in 1921 and became a yearly event to raise funds for charity.

This page and facing page top: A scoundrelly bunch of cut-throat pirates challenges the authority of the Admiral of the Port and his appointed jury, the dreaded skull and crossbones adorning the sail of the pirate ship *(above)*. In its early years, the custom of the 'Beating of the Bounds' had no connection with pirates, either real or fictional, and was a serious event which concentrated on matters such as customs duty, legal problems, and infringements of the regulations. By the 17th century, however, the ceremony had developed into something of a holiday, scheduled to take place each Whit Monday. The day's events, as well as beating the bounds, included landing at Sandbanks for games and a picnic, followed by a memorable evening at an inn. The inclusion of a

boat-load of rascally pirates was a much later addition to the fun and frolics, and it was their involvement that swelled the coffers as they toured the streets of the town demanding cash for charity. No shopkeeper or pub landlord escaped their attentions, and one memorable year they invaded the London Hotel, captured the landlord's wife and a barmaid, and held them to ransom, tied to a post in High Street! Watched eagerly by bystanders on the quay (some of whom were obviously a coach party, parked near the Shipwright's Arms), the pirate ship and the Admiralty vessel draw alongside each other. No shots appear to have been exchanged between the warring sides - though perhaps a few verbal exchanges were made *(facing page, bottom)*! A flotilla of small boats, suitably decorated for the event, followed the boat carrying the Mayor and his party, and the jury's vessel, as they toured the traditional boundaries. The day's fun ended with the capture of the pirates - and the solemn judgment of their 'crimes' by the Mayor. Their sentence, of course, became a tradition in itself: they were condemned to walk the plank - though there was a notable lack of sharks in the harbour to squabble over the 'bodies' of the offenders!

Below: The coronation in June 1953 gave everyone a chance to declare their loyalty to the Queen - and it was party time in Poole. Garlands and banners were hung in windows, lines of bunting stretched across every street, and though the weather on the big day was inclined to be cool and rather damp, it didn't stop the children from enjoying their street parties. This particular party was held in King Street, and some - though unfortunately not all - of the names are known. Mr Cull is the gentleman standing at the back, placing a crown on the head of Janet Barfoot (now Essam). Others whose names are remembered include Audrey Sanson, Geoffrey Barfoot, Michael Guildy, Malcolm Sonner, John Barfoot, and Robert and Colin Sansom. Note the television set significantly placed at the end of the table. This was the first time a coronation had ever been filmed, and those without a TV set crowded into the parlours of their more fortunate neighbours to watch the coronation.

Television was relatively new in the early 1950s, and for those who were privileged to be among those early viewers, the Queen's coronation, even viewed in black and white, was an unforgettable sight.

Each float had its own theme, and many and varied were the subjects tackled that day, ranging from the totally light-hearted to themes that were frivolous on the surface, while at the same time carrying a serious underlying message. That would seem to be the case with the youngsters being carried atop one of Reliance Scrap Metal Merchants' vehicles, who were robots, taking over the jobs once carried out by human beings *(facing page).* The solitary 'human being' sitting at the rear of the float declares that he is 'redundent'. In the jobs market it could be suspected that the young man's spelling abilities might have some bearing on his circumstances....

An enthusiastic though unlikely 'West Indian' band pass the photographer *(top),* introducing themselves and their ingenious home-made instruments as the 'Trinidad Crazy Band'. The band would more than likely have been miming to foot-tapping steel drum music, played through loudspeakers as the vehicle moved along. And around a decade away from Neil Armstrong and 'Buzz' Aldrin's 'giant leap for mankind' of July 1969, half a dozen young men fulfil their fondest ambitions - at least for an hour or two - and become astronauts for the occasion *(above).* A nicely-painted and well-imagined background sets their space ship on some distant and mountainous planet - a float calculated to please every boy between five and fifteen.

Both pages: How many readers will perhaps recognise themselves in one of these scenes from a long-ago Poole Carnival? Great fun was obviously had by all in this particular 1950s parade, and the ingenious costumes and decorations would have been planned out weeks beforehand. DIY enthusiasts would have thrown themselves into constructing the props, while the sewing machines of those mothers and sisters who were handy with a needle would have been buzzing for quite some time. This kind of discrimination was a fact of life even as recently as the 1950s; women had their domestic chores, the blokes wielded the hammer and nails, and few people broke the mould. Readers would no doubt agree, however, that the results of all their hard work were quite spectacular, and as the parade of colourful floats slowly made its way through the streets of Poole, hundreds of local residents and visitors turned out to watch and join in the fun.

Down on the beach

Both pictures: These wonderful images will bring back to our readers those many carefree days spent on the beach at Sandbanks. The tide was out on this hot summer's day, giving the visitors a wide expanse of beach to spread out on *(main picture)*. Even so, it was rather crowded - a definite bonus for the cafe serving coffees and afternoon tea. It is interesting to note that many of the ladies have come out dressed in their posh frocks and smart hats, though the day is warm enough to tempt the younger end into swimming costumes and sunsuits. Today's informal wear still lay far in the future; gentlemen would not be seen in the street without a tie and a hat of some kind, while ladies occasionally wore trousers, the fashion was still widely frowned upon in many circles. The beach, however, was different, and Sandbanks was definitely the place to let your hair down!

Before the 1920s, Sandbanks still had an atmosphere of desolate beauty, which was only beginning to be appreciated. That was the time to buy land, and a few speculators recognised the possibilities of Sandbanks and snapped up plots of land there for £200 to £300. With Brownsea Island on the horizon, the last vehicle appears to have just driven aboard the 'floating bridge' ferry *(inset)*. The steam ferry moved back and forth across the channel by the means of two chains, and because the vessel's bows and stern were identical, a black ball was raised on the end which was going forward to show other ships which way the ferry was travelling. Not everyone arrived by ferry, however; in the 1920s a bus service was started between the Haven Hotel, which lay just off to the right of the photograph, and Poole.

Left: What can be more exciting to kiddies than sand to dig in and waves to splash around in? At least, of course, in those simple days before expensive computer games and videos kept children chained to a flickering screen! The simple pleasures of summer were enough for these youngsters. A sensible sun hat protects one little girl who also appears to be wearing rompers - an item of kiddies' clothing which has entirely vanished from our modern wardrobe. She could well be envied by her big brother who, lacking a swim suit has had make do with the next best option, and roll up his trouser legs. The young mums in this 1930s view are dressed to suit the summer weather; not so the older lady behind them. In her dark hat and heavy, long-sleeved jacket and skirt, she is taking no chances with any cool breeze that might suddenly get up. Though we have no date for the photograph, we can take it for granted that this lady believes in the old adage, 'Ne'er cast a clout till May is out'!

Below: This is one ball you wouldn't have hit very far with a cricket bat! The Sunday Dispatch - now defunct - had generously provided this enormous ball at Branksome Chine, and bathers of all ages found it an irresistible attraction, whether they were pushing it around or trying unsuccessfully to climb on it.

This delightful scene dates from the 1930s or possibly even earlier, and the children who had such a good time that day will since then have lived a lifetime of experiences. Did they bring their own children to enjoy the sea at Branksome Chine, we wonder?

The style of swimwear has changed more than a little since the date of the photograph; the men are still sporting all-in-one costumes with shoulder-straps, while 'modest' would understate the dress of the ladies and young girls. Bikinis, of course, were undreamed of back then. It was 1946 when the skimpy costumes were created by French designer Louis Reard, and the daring new swimwear that revealed flesh hitherto unseen in public was immediately labelled indecent and immodest....If they could see us now! Swimming caps like the one worn here, usually made of white rubber and with an uncomfortable strap that fastened under the chin, were customary among the ladies, and remained popular until recent years.

Golden Years of POOLE

To quote a proverb, there is nothing new under the sun - and a bronzed body was every bit as important in the late 1930s as it is today! Clear blue skies and hot sunshine, a comfortable deckchair - and a pretty girl or a handsome hunk to chat with - Branksome Chine had everything on the day this holiday scene was captured by a passing photographer, and a long row of deck chairs lines the sun terrace overlooking the beach - less of a problem for those who prefer not to get sand in their hair or their shoes - and definitely the right place to work on that tan. Those who revel in the feel of sand between their toes have claimed their

own few yards of space on the beach, where they can put up their deck chairs or lay out their towels and relax in the sun.
There was no big town nightlife here, though the natural beauty of Branksome Chine and its many attractions made this the perfect setting for the kind of unhurried lifestyle sought after by its many visitors.

Events of the 1950s

WHAT'S ON?
Television hit Britain in a big way during the 1950s. Older readers will surely remember 'Double Your Money, Dixon of Dock Green and 'Dragnet' (whose characters' names were changed 'to protect the innocent'). Commercial television was introduced on 22nd September 1955, and Gibbs SR toothpaste were drawn out of the hat to become the first advert to be shown. Many believed adverts to be vulgar, however, and audiences were far less than had been hoped for.

GETTING AROUND
The year 1959 saw the development of the world's first practical air-cushion vehicle - better known to us as the hovercraft. The earliest model was only able to travel at slow speeds over very calm water and was unable to carry more than three passengers. The faster and smoother alternative to the sea ferry quickly caught on, and by the 1970s a 170-ton car-carrying hovercraft service had been introduced across the English Channel.

SPORTING CHANCE
The four-minute mile had remained the record since 1945, and had become regarded as virtually unbreakable. On 6th May 1954, however, Oxford University student Roger Bannister literally ran away with the record, accomplishing the seemingly impossible in three minutes 59.4 seconds. Bannister collapsed at the end of his last amazing lap, even temporarily losing his vision. By the end of the day, however, he had recovered sufficiently to celebrate his achievement in a London night club!

Birds eye view

> *The Haven Hotel was for many years favoured by the stars of stage and screen*

Pleasant woods, sandy dells, a long strip of golden sands, the sun reflected in the blue waters of the bay - all added to the quiet beauty of Sandbanks. The splendid Haven Hotel, built in 1898 when the area was quite undeveloped, was for many years favoured by the stars of stage and screen, and by wealthy yachtsmen. Its other claim to fame was as the place chosen by Guglielmo Marconi for his early experiments with radio signals. The hotel had a major facelift in 1926 (and further major renovations much later, in the late 1970s), and it had much to offer the more sophisticated holiday-maker. Golf, tennis, riding, boating, fishing, dancing, motoring and bathing were all listed by the management as special attractions. Sea views from almost every bedroom, private balconies, sea water baths - all added to the hotel's modern conveniences, and in the late 1930s a room at the Haven would have cost you 27/6d a day (around £1.38p).

Readers will spot in the foreground of this bird's eye view the remains of Harvey's pier, which was destroyed (by our own side!) during the second world war. The Haven tea rooms are nearby to the right - and on the right edge of the photograph we see that the ferry is just approaching the landing stage.

Before the first bridge was built people had to either cross the bay by boat or trek all the way around

From a position far above the rooftops and chimneys of the power station - only five years old when an aerial photographer captured this view in 1958 - we can see that Poole Bridge is in its raised position to allow shipping to pass. Seven times a day, from 9.30 in the morning to 9.30 every evening, traffic between Poole and Hamworthy comes to a halt as vessels pass through. Before the first bridge (made of wood) was built in the 19th century, it was a case of 'so near and yet so far'. People either had to cross by boat or make the long trek around the bay - a fact which makes us thankful for the bridge we have today. Part of the power station, a collection of warehouses and woodyards are in the foreground of the photograph, while the gas works can be seen towards the top of the picture; the gas holder in the left corner is of course no longer with us. The tower of St James' church can be easily picked out in the centre of the old town. The present church was built in 1820, though God has been worshipped on this same spot since the 12th century.

Events of the 1950s

HOT OFF THE PRESS

The 1950s seemed to be the heyday of spies, and in 1951 the activities of Guy Burgess and Donald Maclean caused a sensation in the country. Both had occupied prominent positions in the Foreign Office, while Burgess had also been a member of MI-6. Recruited by the Russians while at Cambridge University in the 1930s, the traitors provided the Soviets with a huge amount of valuable information. They disappeared in 1951, surfacing in Moscow five years later.

THE WORLD AT LARGE

Plans to develop the economies of member states into one common market came to fruition on 1st January 1958, when the EEC came into operation. The original members were France, Belgium, Luxembourg, The Netherlands, Italy, and West Germany. The Community became highly successful, achieving increased trade and prosperity across Western Europe while at the same time alleviating fear of war which lingered on after the end of World War II. Britain became a member in 1973.

SCIENCE AND DISCOVERY

DNA (deoxyribonucleic acid) was first defined as long ago as 1953, and the effects have been far-reaching. The key discovery was developed over the following years and today DNA fingerprinting has become an accepted part of life. Genetic diseases such as hemophilia and cystic fibrosis have been identified. Criminals are continually detected and brought to justice. Biological drugs have been developed. More controversially, drought and disease-resistant plants have been engineered - and Dolly the sheep has been produced.

The twin chimneys of the Power Station immediately attract the eye in this aerial photograph of Poole. Visible for miles around from the land as well as sea, the 325 ft chimneys were an unmistakable landmark. The station, which was completed in 1953, took five years to build yet lasted a mere 40 years. No Fred Dibnah-like lighting of fires was used in the demolition of

the famous octagonal chimneys in 1999; 80lbs of explosive was used to bring the chimneys down, and an astonishing crowd of 10,000 turned out to watch as they crashed to the earth. St James' church, the Quay and Poole Bridge can be easily picked out towards the right, while the character of Hamworthy has changed with the redevelopments of recent years. The line of LCTs (landing craft tanks), used for the D-Day landings, sunk to act as a breakwater after World War II, have disappeared, and the Brittany and Condor high speed ferry terminals have been built since the date of the photograph.

This eagle's eye view of Poole reveals exactly how much the town has changed over the years, especially around the harbour. The railway line can be easily picked out, though since the date of this photograph the ferry terminal has transformed the right foreground of the picture into a hive of activity. On the left near the Poole Yacht Club the pier reaches seawards from Lower Hamworthy. Poole Lifting Bridge just intrudes into the left edge of the scene, while bang in the centre of the town is St James' church, a landmark which few will fail to recognise. Not too far away along the Quayside we can pick out

the colonnades of the old Harbour Office - built in 1822 - which became the premises of HM Coastguard and Fisheries. Across Thames Street is The Town Cellars, built in the 1430s as a wool warehouse, today housing the Maritime Museum and Tourist Information Office. Further to the right, the Customs House is a much later building, a replica of a replica of the Red Lion Coffee House, which once stood on the same spot. To the right of the 12th century church of St James, the line of High Street, featured in detail in a number of photographs, leads away diagonally towards the top corner.

Around the harbour

'Messing about in boats' is an occupation dear to the hearts of the people of Poole, whether their interest lies in weekend sailing or in a career aboard one of the larger craft which regularly visited the quay. In the distance is Poole bridge, a familiar landmark for many years, and those who regularly travel between Poole and Hamworthy would find it difficult to imagine life without it. There was a time, however, when bridging the gap was merely a distant dream. The plan to build a bridge was proposed in 1833, welcomed warmly by the many who realised that such a facility would clip two miles off their journey - an important consideration in the day when the horse and cart reigned supreme. The proposal, however, was fiercely opposed by those who feared that Poole's narrow streets would become congested with traffic, but in 1834 the Poole Bridge Bill was passed. The first toll bridge, built from wood at a cost of £9,600, had a steep gradient which posed a problem for horses. Its centre span, which swung open for the passage of ships, was hand operated. In 1885 a second bridge, this time of iron, replaced it, and in 1926 Poole Council purchased the bridge, abolished the tolls, and replaced it with a third - the present bridge - which was opened a year later.

Right: Stacks of sawn timber await unloading in this quayside scene, which is made all the more fascinating by the equipment used (you don't see derricks like this one any more), the old three-wheeled truck, and the marvellous little car in the foreground, which some

knowledgeable reader will immediately identify. The car, which bears a local registration number, also presents a small mystery: why does it have a Union Jack mounted in front of its radiator? Does this perhaps signify some recent royal event? We will never know.

The derricks aboard the vessel have already been hard at work, winching the timber from ship to shore on to the waiting trailer. 'American Hardwoods' is the name on the cab door; they dealt in fencing, doors and wall boards. There is an almost readable sign mounted on the trailer itself, perhaps Laycock Ltd of Bournemouth.

It was the middle of the last century when Poole became a key centre for building materials - mainly due to the expansion of nearby Bournemouth - and a number of local firms grew up in Poole to specialise in importing timber. Poole's imports did not stop at timber; other building materials such as drainpipes, roofing materials, bricks and slate were also brought in through Poole.

Below: Viewed from the grounds of the Haven Hotel, the Haven Tea Rooms, far right, were just the place for day visitors and holidaymakers to enjoy a pot of tea and a snack - and, of course, that essential ingredient of every pleasant day out, ice cream. The car ferry, unusually quiet at the time, lies at the landing stage ready for the next journey across the channel.

Brimming with character, Sandbanks has always been the perfect place to unwind; take a stroll, have fun in the sun, or simply bask in the sunshine. The area was beginning to be developed at the time of the photograph, but at the turn of the 20th century its value as a popular resort was just being realised. Apart from the Haven Hotel there was little in the way of building development, and a collection of wooden shacks and railway carriages had been erected as summer houses. Today, the beautiful beaches of Sandbanks possess the coveted Blue Flag award.

Brownsea Island, dominating the skyline, would not have been open to visitors at the time; the general public were not welcome on the privately owned island. It was opened to the public in 1963 and today the natural beauty of its heath and woodland can be enjoyed by anyone.

Events of the 1950s

MELODY MAKERS

Few teenage girls could resist the blatant sex-appeal of 'Elvis the Pelvis', though their parents were scandalised at the moody Presley's provocatively gyrating hips. The singer took America and Britain by storm with such hits as 'Jailhouse Rock', 'All Shook Up' and 'Blue Suede Shoes'. The rhythms of Bill Haley and his Comets, Buddy Holly and Chuck Berry turned the 1950s into the Rock 'n' Roll years.

INVENTION AND TECHNOLOGY

Until the late 1950s you did not carry radios around with you. Radios were listened to at home, plugged into a mains socket in every average sitting room. Japan was in the forefront of electronic developments even then, and in 1957 the Japanese company Sony introduced the world's very first all-transistor radio - an item of new technology that was small enough to fit into your pocket. The major consumer product caught on fast - particularly with teenage listeners.

ROYAL WATCH

King George VI's health had been causing problems since 1948, when he developed thrombosis. In 1951 the King - always a heavy smoker - became ill again, and was eventually found to be suffering from lung cancer. His left lung was removed in September of 1951. In January 1952 he waved Princess Elizabeth and Prince Philip off on their tour of Africa; they were never to see him again. The King died in the early hours of 6th February 1952.

The compleat anglers....but did these young fishermen catch anything? There will be more than one reader who will remember their own youth, when they spent Saturdays and school holidays doing exactly the same thing. Playing out was far safer back then; life was more active, and entertainment was not linked to computer games and television.

The photograph was taken sometime during the 1930s, and the boys who fished on the quay that day will be in their 70s today. Gives you a creepy feeling, doesn't it? Will they perhaps be among our readers, and recognise themselves, we wonder? Nearby, a rather nice private yacht is moored at the quayside. Alongside is a sailing boat, and the dinghy alongside indicates that there is someone aboard. In the background is Newman's boatyard. After being closed and empty for a number of years it was bought in the late 1990s by Sunseeker Boats.

Both pictures: In spite of the open sun roof in the foreground, the day chosen for the boat racing, if we can judge by the number of coats and hats, was rather cool *(below)*. Nevertheless, the rain has obviously held off, and people have turned out in their hundreds to watch the events of the day. This is a true family event, and parents with toddlers and young children in tow, some of them pushing prams, hurry to the quayside to obtain the best view possible. We can see by the row of cycles parked in the train lines that not a few of them have arrived on two wheels; those were the gentler days when you could leave your bike at the pavement edge or outside a shop and expect to find it still there on your return! Others have come by car, and the somewhat haphazard parking along the Quay would no doubt have raised the temperatures of those who returned to their vehicles to find themselves hemmed in (though 'road rage' still lay many decades in the future!). The London to Cowes race, organised by the Royal Motor Yacht Club, was an annual event that involved cruisers such as these vessels moored at Poole Quay *(right)*. Today, the emphasis is on tourism, and since the time of these photographs many changes have come to the Quay. Though as busy now as in earlier years, attractions such as the aquarium, the potteries tour, music and fireworks are as likely to be experienced by summer visitors as those connected with boats and the sea.

Golden Years of POOLE

This was the Cowes to Poole cruiser race - the date is unfortunately unknown - and in gala mood, those participating in the weekend racing have raised a fine display of colourful bunting to flutter gaily in the breeze. The race was organised by the Royal Motor Yacht Club from their headquarters at Poole Quay,

though the many local clubs such as the Hamworthy and Bournemouth Sailing Club and the Parkstone Yacht Club each organised their own races. The sailing season, which ran through the summer months between May and September, saw not only the big annual regattas but boat races from Poole to

64

Cherbourg, Normandy and Ouistreham, and nearer home, the Isle of Wight, Brixham and Weymouth. Thanks to its natural harbour, Poole has a long seagoing history, and as the emphasis shifted from industry to leisure the town made every effort to attract yachtsmen, from the many ship chandlers to the expert help and advice offered by the Harbour Office.

Events of the 1960s

WHAT'S ON?
Television comedy came into its own in the 1960s, and many of the shows that were favourites then went on to become classics. 'On the Buses', 'Steptoe and Son', 'Till Death Us Do Part' and 'The Army Game' kept audiences laughing, while the incredible talents of Morecambe and Wise, the wit of Des O'Connor - often the butt of the duo's jokes - and the antics of Benny Hill established them for ever in the nation's affections.

GETTING AROUND
The 2nd March 1969 was a landmark in the history of aviation. The Anglo-French supersonic airliner Concorde took off for the first time from Toulouse in France. Concorde, which can cruise at almost twice the speed of sound, was designed to fly from London to New York in an incredible three hours twenty minutes. The event took place just weeks after the Boeing 747, which can carry 500 passengers to Concorde's modest 100, made its first flight.

SPORTING CHANCE
Wembley Stadium saw scenes of jubilation when on 30th July 1966 England beat West Germany 4-2 in the World Cup. The match, played in a mixture of sunshine and showers, had been a nailbiting experience for players and spectators alike from the very beginning when Germany scored only thirteen minutes into the game. It was Geoff Hurst's two dramatic goals scored in extra time that secured the victory and lifted the cup for England - at last.

Above: A wide expanse of placid water dotted with a variety of small craft, gardens of almost tropical greenery - this could almost be a scene from the Riviera or the Cote d'Azur. It is, however, the entrance to the Sandbanks Pavilion - showing us yet again just what beauties Poole had - and still has - to offer. Across the bay readers will be able to pick out the Royal Motor Yacht Club, a key mover in Poole's boat racing activities. On the skyline lies the historic Brownsea Island, which saw the birth of the Boy Scout movement back in 1907. During the 1920s the island became the property of Mrs Christie. At first she tolerated visitors to the island, but after a bad experience she banned uninvited guests from landing on her shores - sadly, including the boy scouts. It was 1963 before the island opened again, and for a fee of a mere half a crown visitors could land and explore the delights of Brownsea, many of them for the very first time. The road was virtually empty on the day of the photograph, and a solitary A55 Austin Cambridge is the only vehicle on the move. The Austin Cambridge was later to evolve and emerge in a new boxy style which was indistinguishable from the Morris Oxford.

Above right: Another strenuous fishing trip has come to an end, and it's time to hang up the nets to dry, strike a light, and sit around on the quay exchanging yarns and smoking a quiet pipe. Unfortunately we have no date for this marvellous photograph which evokes real nostalgia; captured during the era of gas lighting, even the old lamp adds its own particular character to the scene (note the ornamental arms at the top, intended originally to take the lamplighter's ladder). Many readers will recall the days when gas lamps shed their pale light on the streets of Poole; pale, that is, looking back from the kind of lighting we have become used to today, which are brilliant in contrast. Poole's fishing industry dates back hundreds of years. The town's links with Newfoundland date back to the 16th century, when Poole's senior bailiff was fined £30 for deserting his post to embark on a voyage to the 'New founde Land'. He was only the first of many, and by the 19th century Poole's fishing industry was thriving, with 350 ships engaged in the trade.

Right: The sight of Poole Bridge being raised has always attracted the interest of visitors, and this view, probably shot in the mid 1930s, captures a small group of bystanders who have gathered on the quay, waiting either to cross to Hamworthy or simply to watch the 'Nicke' make her way through the cantilevered bridge. The rowing boat and its occupants appears to have taken up a vulnerable position, though it is probably further from the path of the 'Nicke' than would seem from this viewpoint. The ship would no doubt have been offloading coal for the power station. This iron bridge, opened in 1927, was the third to be built between Poole and Hamworthy.

Below: Poole Quay, often a hive of frenetic activity, was a haven of peace when a passing photographer recorded this tranquil scene - a virtual forest of masts - for posterity. Few people were out and about at the time, though a couple of boat owners were aboard, busy, perhaps, with essential maintenance or perhaps simply tidying up. Note the man at the masthead on the left of the photograph! Many years ago the Quay was far smaller than it is today, extending from the Town Cellars to around half way to the Hamworthy Bridge. By the end of the 18th century, however, the Newfoundland trade was still flourishing, and the number of ships using the Quay had risen from around a hundred in the mid 1600s to 300. In response to the growing demand for space, the Quay was improved and lengthened. Hand in hand with the fluctuations in Poole's traditional industries, however, its use changed and today pleasure craft far outnumber those connected with trade and industry.

On the move

Below: Dressed against the chill of a cool day, fish merchant Tom Hockey (who has since passed on) poses proudly for the camera in Lagland Street; the building seen in the background is Norton's Library. A box of fish lies hidden beneath a cover on the barrow, which Mr Hockey had ingeniously attached to the back of his bicycle. Towing the barrow, he would do the rounds of the streets of Poole, his loud cries of 'Fresh fish for sale!' attracting customers from their houses. It was rumoured that Tom Hockey had the loudest voice in Poole - an allegation which, for the lack of organised competition, remained unproven, but was probably correct. If his fish-selling business had ever failed, he could perhaps have found a position as town crier! Mr Hockey was one of Poole's more well-known characters, and it is unfortunate that so little is known of the man himself.

It was a good day for an outing, and in the days when workers had shorter holidays, few days off, and less disposable income, the occasional day trip was eagerly looked forward to. This smart white charabanc is well loaded: was it really capable of carrying upwards of 35 passengers as well as the driver? Everyone has turned out in their Sunday best, with flowery hats and smart clothes. It would be nice to know where these trippers were bound for; were they heading off to Blandford, Corfe Castle, or the Llama Tree Gardens? Or were they going further afield to Brockenhurst, Beaulieu or Cerne Abbas? Many of the early 'charas' (though probably not this one) served a dual purpose; during the week they acted as delivery vehicles, then when the weekend came, rows of seats were added ready for those trips to the seaside that became popular with office and shop workers during the 1920s and 30s. The trips offered a great day out at a reasonable price, and once the charabanc was bowling along the sun and wind would blow any workaday blues away. The vehicle was convertible, and in the event of rain the fold-down hood would be hastily fixed in place.

Events of the 1960s

MELODY MAKERS

The 1960s: those were the days when the talented blues guitarist Jimi Hendrix shot to rock stardom, a youthful Cliff Richard charmed the nation with his 'Congratulations' and Sandie Shaw won the Eurovision Song Contest for Britain with 'Puppet on a String'. It was the combined musical talents of a group of outrageous working-class Liverpool lads, however, who formed the Beatles and took the world by storm with music that ranged from the experimental to ballads such as 'Yesterday'.

INVENTION AND TECHNOLOGY

A major step forward was made in 1960 when the laser was invented. An acronym for Light Amplification by Stimulated Emission of Radiation, the device produces a narrow beam of light that can travel for vast distances and is focused to give enormous power. Laser beams, as well as being able to carry far more information than radio waves, can also be used for surgery, cutting, drilling, welding and scores of other operations.

SCIENCE AND DISCOVERY

When the drug Thalidomide was first developed during the 1950s it was hailed as a wonder drug which would ease the distressing symptoms of pregnancy sickness. By the early 1960s the drug's terrible side effects were being discovered, when more than 3000 babies had been born with severe birth defects. Malformed limbs, defective eyes and faulty intestines were the heart-rending legacy left by Thalidomide.

Poole Park lake - an impressive sight that greets visitors arriving from London by train - covers an amazing 60 acres. It was a quiet, sunny day, probably during the 1930s, when this view was caught on camera; did the motor cycle leaning against the tree perhaps belong to the photographer? The original Victorian benches, seen here in a shady spot beneath

the tree, were to eventually disappear, though happily, as part of the park's centenary celebrations in 1990, similar seats were reinstated. Poole Park has been delighting local people and visitors alike for many years, whether it is to play cricket or tennis, sail boats (though not, in the early 20th century, on Sunday afternoons!), picnic on the wide stretches of grass, or to simply stroll on a pleasant summer afternoon. A number of vehicles can be seen in the photograph, and in spite of the eight miles per hour speed limit traffic was set to become a real problem over the years.

Right: The ferry to Studland was very busy when this scene was recorded in the late 1940s, and not all of the queuing vehicles - some of them obviously outside the range of the photographer's viewfinder - will find room on the ferry this time around! An official aboard the waits to guide each of the drivers into a safe position, as close together as space will allow. A row of cars parked in the foreground are here to enjoy Sandbanks itself rather than to take a trip to Corfe Castle or Swanage. If the number plates are anything to go by, the owners are holidaying here from far afield: CTW 943 was registered in Essex, while ABN 443 is far from its original stamping ground of Bolton in Lancashire.

The so-called 'floating bridge' was built in 1926 at a cost of £12,000, and served Poole well until it was taken out of service in 1958 and replaced by a modern ferry. Many readers will remember the old steam ferry, however, and will perhaps still retain a soft spot for it.

Below: A trickle of light traffic waits in Bournemouth Road, Parkstone, to turn right into Poole Road. There is little sign here of the level of traffic that was set to increase gradually in the second half of the 20th century. In the background of the photograph is the Sharp, Jones & Co's pottery, whose outbuildings and pipe yard extended far behind, along Cromer Road. When the company was set up back in 1853 this area was heathland, with little promise back then of the huge pottery and concrete works - the very first in England - that was to evolve over the years. Pottery has been made in the area for hundreds of years; in fact it was its local clay (recognised back in 1791 by pottery king Josiah Wedgwood of Burslem, Stoke on Trent) which was to save Poole from the general decline in trade that hit the town during the early years of the 19th century. Steam tugs with a loaded barges strung out behind regularly left Poole Quay, bound for Liverpool. Interestingly, the barges made the return journey loaded with timber from the Baltics and slate from Welsh quarries, making the trip well worthwhile.

At the time of this photograph, the Seaforth offered hot and cold water - a very up-to-date facility

Adverts for hotels and businesses in Swanage and even the Isle of Wight offer these holiday-makers plenty of choice as, with the Haven Hotel framing the background, they set out from Sandbanks on the well-used ferry to Swanage. Readers will perhaps remember similar journeys made at the time, in just such 'sit up and beg' cars as these marvellous old vehicles. They may even be able to remember how much they paid for the crossing! The camera catches an official as he collects his fares from the waiting drivers. For some of them, this would be a pleasant day out; others would have come from further afield, and would perhaps have been looking forward to their annual two-week holiday in the pleasant seaside town for many months. Would they be staying at the Seaforth Private Hotel in Victoria Avenue, we wonder? As we can see from the advert on the right, the Seaforth offered visitors hot and cold water in each of its bedrooms - a very up-to-date facility at the time, and one which was definitely not available in all seaside 'digs'!

At work

This page: A scene that will stir memories, though younger readers will perhaps have trouble pinpointing the location *(below right)*. With Ashley Road in the foreground, continuing into Poole Road, the Sharp, Jones pottery can just be seen on the far left of the photograph behind the rather attractive three-gabled building. Could this building perhaps have been the firm's original premises? There was little development in the area when Sharp, Jones & Co set up business here in 1853 to manufacture bricks and pipes. Before World War II, many of Sharp, Jones's pipes were used for drainage for new housing developments. A change of direction came with the declaration of war in 1939, however; around the country new airfields were hastily built, all of which needed drainage, and this involved large government contracts being taken on by the company. Work carried out involved the manufacture of huge quantities of dummy torpedoes for use in military training. Unlike many more unlucky factories, Sharp, Jones & Co escaped serious damage during the war; a number of incendiaries fell on the plant, but the damage they caused was minimal. By the 1950s the plant was employing around 140 local men in the various processes, in what had become the most modern concrete plant in

Britain. The wheels of time move on, however, and in 1982 the factory was demolished. On the same spot today you can shop at the modern premises of Sainsbury's Homebase, and browse among the home furnishings at Courts and MFI. In the second view, which looks in the opposite direction *(bottom)*, a heavily loaded lorry has just turned from Poole Road into Bournemouth Road; note the sun blinds shading the windows of the shop on the corner, which carry an advert for Bourne Radio. The Sharp, Jones pottery just edges into the photograph on the far right.

This page and overleaf: Women have long been extensively employed in the pottery industry, from fettling to quality assessment. The better paid workers were the paintresses, whose artistic skills and keen eye for fine detail made them the creme de la creme among the workforce. Towards the end of the 19th century the company which would one day become Poole Pottery were already establishing themselves as a force to be reckoned with, and by the early years of the 20th century they were producing hand painted pottery. Using the traditional Delft technique, they painted on to the unfired glaze, developing the distinctive style which came to typify Poole Pottery's decorative ware. Christine Lucas *(previous page)* is adding the vital finishing touch, banding and spotting - a skill which requires a keen eye and an exceptionally steady hand.

The second photograph shows a number of young paintresses hard at work in the studio at Poole Pottery.

Working in the good light from a row of windows, these ladies are adding the designs to a range of tableware, painting on to the unfired glaze in the traditional manner *(below)*.

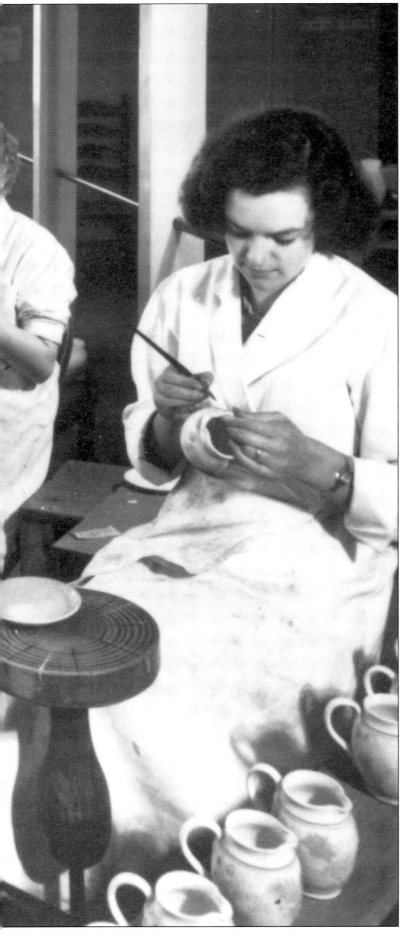

Events of the 1960s

HOT OFF THE PRESS
Barbed wire, concrete blocks and a wide no-man's-land divided East from West when a reinforced wall was built right across the city of Berlin in 1961. Many East Germans escaped to the West at the eleventh hour, taking with them only the possessions they could carry. The Berlin Wall divided the city - and hundreds of family members and friends - for 28 years until the collapse of Communist rule across Eastern Europe. Who can ever forget those scenes in 1989, when ordinary people themselves began to physically tear down the hated wall?

THE WORLD AT LARGE
'One giant leap for mankind' was taken on 20th July 1969, when Neil Armstrong made history as the first man to set foot on the moon. During the mission he and fellow-astronaut 'Buzz' Aldrin collected rock and soil samples, conducted scientific experiments - and had a lot of fun jumping around in the one-sixth gravity. Twenty-one hours and thirty-seven minutes after their landing they took off again in their lunar module 'Eagle' to rejoin Apollo II which was orbiting above them, proudly leaving the American flag on the Moon's surface.

ROYAL WATCH
Princess Margaret's announcement in 1960 that she was to wed photographer Antony Armstrong-Jones (later Lord Snowdon) brought sighs of relief from her immediate family. Just five years earlier the people of Britain had sympathised as the princess bowed to public and private pressure, ending her relationship with Peter Townsend, Prince Philip's former equerry. The Church (and the Queen, as its Head) frowned on the liaison as Townsend was divorced. Her marriage to Lord Snowdon itself ended in 1978.

Both pictures: Young, pretty - and very talented, Poole Pottery's Gertie Gilham hand throws a pot in the traditional way used by potters for many centuries *(below)*. Note the fixed markers on the right of the photograph; these were used to ensure that all the vases of this particular design were exactly the same. The top marker indicates the height it should be, while the bottom two prescribe the width of the vase. Far from being as easy as it looks, hand throwing is a skill which has to be painstakingly acquired - as many who have tried it, and have only succeeded in producing a shapeless lump of clay, have discovered. Children visiting the pottery's craft village today can have a go at throwing their own pots - an education in itself. Slip casting of hollow shapes such as teapots and vases like this one being made by Gertie Gilham is a technique often used today. Liquid clay or 'slip' is poured into moulds, left to set, then fired.

The huge, modern electric kilns reach an incredible temperature of 1060 , and the equipment as well as the method is very different from that used at the time this pottery worker loaded glazed ware into the kiln many years ago *(right)*. We can't be sure what temperature this kiln reached, but it would have taken between 12 and 24 hours to fire the pottery.

Seizing the window of opportunity

The friendship between Arthur Tombs and Ralph Crocker began whilst they were working for 'Brown's Glass of Boscombe' during the 1930s. This friendship was to prove to be a prerequisite for the existence of 'The Dorset Glass Company Ltd' as it is known today.

Before gaining their jobs at 'Brown's Glass' Arthur had trained as a Lead Light Designer at the Royal College of Art whilst Ralph had trained as a Glazier. With the advent of the second world war however, Arthur left the company in order to join the Royal Navy and bravely serve his country. Ralph, who had served in the first world war until he was invalided, was by now too old to serve in the second world war and so took over Arthur's job in his absence. After the cessation of the

war the glass industry, like so many other industries at this time, experienced a shortage of materials. This was partly caused because government policy, expressed through the Export Council, stated that business in export markets must not be refused in order to satisfy any non-essential home demand. Therefore, when Arthur went back to 'Brown's Glass' in 1946, after being demobbed from the Royal Navy, he was faced with the news that there were no jobs available at the company.

Ralph and Arthur's friendship stood this test and in fact resulted in becoming stronger than ever. Arthur insisted that Ralph keep the job as he was older and so needed it more than him. In turn Ralph insisted that Arthur have the job back as he had two younger children that he needed to support. After much discussion the friends reached a compromise.

They made the decision to set up their own business together in partnership, contributing £200 each. It was then, in the April of 1946, that 'The Dorset Glass Company' was established.

A converted stables and hayloft, situated in Denmark Lane at Longfleet, the old part of Poole, became the location of Arthur and Ralph's burgeoning business. Indeed, the company remained at this site for 22 years. The initial years of the new business were successful ones. The local authority housing and Ministry of Defence carried out post-war redevelopment in the area. This rebuilding of Poole after the war meant that there was plenty of work for Arthur and Ralph and they were able to take on their first employee paying a weekly wage of 7/6 pence!

Only five years after 'The Dorset Glass Company' was established Arthur and Ralph were able to make the company limited and in 1951, proudly re-named it as, 'The Dorset Glass Company Ltd.'. The early part of this decade had yet more success in store for the friends' company. The most important event in the history of 'The Dorset Glass Company Ltd.' until the 1970s, occurred during these years. Arthur and Ralph's company became one of only 19 companies in the country to be an account handler with Pilkington, the glass company.

On Monday June 24th 1957, 'The Dorset Glass Company Ltd' temporarily departed from its premises at Denmark Lane. The company moved to West Quay Road in Poole whilst the old premises underwent a refurbishment. The workshops and offices in Denmark Lane were rebuilt and during this time the company sent notices to their clients informing them of the temporary move and reassuring them that they would not experience any inconvenience during the reorganisation. Just over seven months later, on Monday

February 3rd 1958, 'The Dorset Glass Company Ltd' resumed residency at their original premises in Denmark Lane and again, made sure that their clients were duly informed of their return.

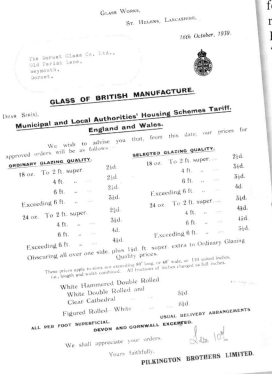

During the years following the return to Denmark Lane, 'The Dorset Glass Company Ltd' continued to thrive and indeed, continued to build up its reputation as a recognised centre for the supply of every type of glass and window frame demanded by the builders throughout the fast developing area in and around Poole.

Amongst many of their successful product lines was what was called, 'The County Range of Mirrors'. This range comprised of differently designed mirrors each named after a county, for instance, there was a 'Devon' mirror, a 'Derby' mirror, a 'Rutland' mirror and so on. This range was advertised as, 'a selection of modern and traditional designs with a style to suit every room decor'. The mirrors were made from the best quality quarter inch plate glass and silvered by the firm's experienced craftsman. Another popular range at this time was the firm's 'Frameless Glass Show Cases and Display Units' range which again came in a variety of designs which could be adapted to meet the client's requirements and which were advertised as, 'Modern and Hygienic"!

Arthur and Ralph were joined in their flourishing business by their sons. Ralph had one son, Brian Crocker who joined the firm in 1950 and was involved in the business until he reached his 50's. Arthur had two sons, Michael and Angus Tombs who joined the firm in 1952 and 1954 respectively. This marked the rise of 'The Dorset Glass Company Ltd' as a family company from its solid origins as a partnership of friends. Michael and Angus are both

Above: *A letter from Pilkington Glass, dated 1939, with their revised price list.* **Left:** *The Denmark Lane premises pictured in the 1950s. Seen in the picture from left to right are Ted Heath, Colin Brazier, Bill Green, Reg Harris and Brian Crocker, son of the co-founder.*

still involved in the business today but in a different capacity from when they first joined. Indeed, they are now both running the company as joint Managing Directors.

After 22 years at Denmark Lane the business moved again, but unlike the brief spell at West Quay Road, this time the move was to be permanent. In 1968, 'The Dorset Glass Company Ltd' became one of the first businesses to purchase land from Poole Council on the new Nuffield Industrial Estate at the Fleets Bridge end of Old Wareham Road. A new factory was built but, the move to the new premises was somewhat less grand than the impressive new building. The main moving procedure took just one weekend and remarkably, the company was ready for business as usual on Monday 8th July.

This expansion and move signalled a new phase in the history of the company and furthered the

Above: An early advertisement. Below: Unloading 6mm float glass.

continuing success of the business. The new premises covered some 14000 square feet on a one acre site. The reception department was situated in the new large showroom which had direct access through the front entrance from the main estate road. Characteristically, the new premises made use of many of the materials that the company was involved with. Profilit structural glass, Pilkington Spectrafloat (a solar reflecting glass) and armour-clad infill panels were used and Plyglass hermetically sealed double glazing was also installed throughout the building. The loading and unloading bays were designed for easy access and exit for vehicles and the most advanced mechanical handling equipment was installed including, a hydraulically operated rotating grab, an overhead crane and a vacuum lifting frame for larger sized of plate glass.

As well as investing in new premises, the company introduced their own new product in this same year. 'The Dorset Glass Company Ltd' took its years of

Tel.: POOLE 967

The Dorset Glass Co. Ltd

DENMARK LANE
POOLE - DORSET

Frameless Glass Show Cases and Display Units

MODERN and HYGIENIC

ALL GLASS USED IS ¼ THICK WITH ALL EDGES POLISHED

experience and knowledge and put them in to practice. In conjunction with other members of the Insulation Glazing Association, they produced their own form of internal double glazing under the name CDK. This new product was designed to ensure simple installation as well as efficiency and low cost. The company advertised their new product and the move to their new premises in the local paper. The caption for the advert was, 'a moving story ... or shall we say a success story?' and it guaranteed that, 'Our service to you will continue - even more efficiently from our new premises. You are cordially invited to visit us!".

This guarantee was achieved and subsequently the company continued to flourish. Ralph Crocker, retired in 1969 aged 66 leaving the thriving company 23 years after co-founding it. Indeed, a year later, only two years on from the move to the Nuffield Industrial Estate, the company was yet again ready to expand further and a new branch was opened in Weymouth in 1970. The year, 1972 also marked a significant development in the history of 'The Dorset Glass Company Ltd'. The long standing account that the company held with Pilkington for glass supplies was no longer exclusive as, in this year, the market opened and glass could be bought worldwide.

After 35 years spent building up the business he co-founded, Arthur Tombs retired in 1981 leaving the company in his sons capable hands. Danny French, Ralph Crocker's grandson joined the company in 1983 and is now the Contracts Director. In 1989, in line with further developments in the company, Michael Tombs

Top: This Southern Railway platform trolley had been used in the works for years and was restored to commemorate the firm's 50th Anniversary.
Right: A Ford Luton van used during the 1980s.

designed and arranged for a new perimeter fence and gates, made by British Steel, to be erected at the company premises. A year later another improvement was made. In compliance with new legislations for safety, the company purchased a fully computerised, automatic laminate glass cutting machine. This purchase, in the summer of 1990, meant that the company was one of the first to own such a machine. Despite this notable event, 1990 will be remembered by 'The Dorset Glass Company Ltd' for different reasons.

1990 was also the year of, what has come to be known as, 'The Great Storm'! The day started normally for the directors of the company who were already engrossed in a Director's Meeting at nine o'clock that morning. However, as the meeting got underway the directors looked up out of the window to see the roof of the adjoining factory crashing towards them. As well as causing much structural damage along the south coast, the storm also managed to blow in a Profilit glass wall at the premises. Luckily, nobody at the company was hurt or injured. In fact, this event actually ended well when the damage was repaired with the most modern glazing materials.

'The Dorset Glass Company Ltd' continued to thrive in the 90's and carried out many projects for clients such as, schools, Dorset County Council, Residents' Associations and private houses. One such project, that stands out amongst the long list of clients, is the fitting of windows, aluminium fabrication curtain walling and patio doors in an ultra-modern house at Sandbanks.

When Arthur Tombs and Ralph Crocker first established their own company in 1946 they hardly dared to imagine that 50 years later the business would still be in existence as a successful family concern. However, 1996 did indeed mark the 50th anniversary of 'The Dorset Glass Company Ltd' and this was a celebratory year for the company. To commemorate the Golden Anniversary a former Southern Railway platform trolley, which had served the company in the works for many years, was carefully restored to its former glory. This time however, under the firm's name was written; 'Glass merchants with vision for 50 years' and the advert on the side of the trolley rightly boasted; 'Our name is your guarantee'. In this anniversary year the number of company employees had risen from one in the beginning to 36, seven of whom were descendants of the two founders. Michael and Angus Tombs organised a dinner and dance for past and present employees and their families at the Marsham Court Hotel in Bournemouth to celebrate this special occasion. Michael was delighted at making

Top right: *Installation taking place in the summer of 1990 of the fully computerised Italian Coopmes automatic laminate glass cutting machine.*
Right: *A new lorry arrives.*

Today, 'The Dorset Glass Company Ltd' is still driving forward with success. The company now holds an operations licence for its lorries as well as owning several small vans. The main markets for the company today are the production of windows and double glazing units and as a glass merchant. In this capacity they supply glass throughout the UK from Manchester to the Channel Isles! Michael's son Crispin currently works for the firm as does Angus' son Duncan as Windows Manager and Sales Director respectively. With the third generation of Tombs now involved in this family business and with their investment in the latest machinery 'The Dorset Glass Company Ltd' are hoping to continue succeed in Poole in the future.

the half-century and stated, 'It is quite an achievement in this day and age ... we get offers to buy us up all the time, but we are not in it to take the money and run. We want to ensure the business for the family'. Indeed, Angus and Michael's father, Arthur Tombs, who co-founded the company and had ensured that the business was passed on to them, attended the 50th anniversary dinner at, by then, the grand age of 85.

Top: *Refurbishment of Parkstone Grammar School.*
Above left: *Installation of Kawneor Architectural Aluminium windows for the National Grid.*

Making waves in Poole's history

Sunseeker International, now the world's largest privately owned and managed motoryacht manufacturer, actually began life from a forecourt garage and car dealership in Christchurch. It was during the early 1960s that Idris Braithwaite decided to buy a little Owens speedboat purely for private family use. However, on visiting the Owens dealership, the skilful salesman, Jeff Tobert, as well as selling a speedboat, persuaded Idris to take on an Owens dealership!

The future Sunseeker business was born and Idris and John Macklin started selling a few runabouts from Friarscliff Garage as a sideline to their motor business. The sales of the boats soared. Soon, a new yard had to be purchased and converted for use as boat storage and a chandlery shop. Indeed, the boat sales soon became the primary concern of the business which changed its name accordingly to Friarscliff Marine.

The burgeoning business flourished and the dealerships of Coronet, Dolphin, Glastron and Fletcher were added to the original Owens dealership. Not content to rest on their laurels Idris and John set themselves the further challenge of building a boat. They successfully completed a wooden craft. Unfortunately, this did not impress the elder Braithwaite son, Robert who had a passion for somewhat faster runabouts. Luckily, just before Owens ceased trading they commissioned a new design of runabout. Robert seized his opportunity and added some refinements to the design to come up with a completely new concept in runabout design; the Sovereign Sports 17!

Right: *Offshore 28.*
Below: *Sovereign Sportsman 17.*

The business was renamed Poole Powerboats to reflect this expansion.

In 1970 Robert and his brother John towed two of the new boats to the Genoa Boat Show. Despite not being able to speak a word of Italian the brothers managed to sell both boats and secure several orders for more! This marked the beginning of the export side of the business. By the end of the year the Sovereign boats were being sold from a dealership network. The dealership in the South of France was owned by a former F1 motor racing driver, Damon Hill's godfather, Henry Taylor. Through Henry, Robert met Don Shead who subsequently came up with some designs for Robert's range of sports cruisers. The boats developed at that time however, were eventually named, Sunseeker, but not before receiving some expressed reservations from the marine journalist, Ray Bulman. The men were testing the latest Sovereign out on an inhospitable day in January when Robert ran

the new name by Ray. Ray responded, 'Sunseeker! In this weather, hells bells! ... Take my advice stick with the garage. That Sunseeker name will never catch on!'. Thankfully, Robert ignored this advice and the new Sunseeker boats were successfully launched at the Paris boat show in 1971 from which, the company has never looked back but continued with its groundbreaking designs.

Indeed, in 1972 at the London Boat Show, it was Henry Taylor again, who initiated another ground breaking design from Sunseeker. He suggested that he would purchase one of the 23 new models the company were promoting but only if it were in white with a full length sun bed. The company's effort to please the customer paid off and the model was built with a sun bed and became a considerable success.

Above: *Rapallo 36.*
Top: *23 Sports.*
Right: *S20.*

By the late 70s, Sunseekers were selling well in the UK and Northern Europe but were not considered stylish enough for the developing Mediterranean market. There still, the only boats selling in any numbers were Scandinavian or Italian as no British company had before tried to compete in such a challenging market place. However, the tantalising Mediterranean market proved to be an irresistible attraction for the innovative company. Apart from the obvious sales potential, the company also saw the value of an overseas market which would help to offset the frequent financial problems experienced in the UK. Sunseekers knew what was needed, it wanted to create boats that would inject a racing frisson into the general boating leisure industry. However, they did not believe that they possessed the necessary skills to achieve the performance standards required. It was then that Don Shead was approached for help with the below-the-waterline physics of an advanced hull design. The most important result of this union was the creation of a relationship that has lasted to this day. The more immediate outcome was the production of the Offshore

28, a radical leap of courage and imagination and the first boat of its kind in Europe. More than 130 Offshore 28s were built, followed by a number of other models, including the Monaco 12m which was Sunseeker's first shaft drive boat. As the company's first really big boat, the Monaco carried engines that seem prehistoric nowadays. The twin MAN V10s delivered what was then a staggering 400hp. Today, three V12 engine of the same size produce 1300hp and much larger boats can reach speeds in excess of 50 knots.

By 1983 the company had continued to develop so much, producing stylish boats and setting new performance standards, that the name was changed once again. The ever increasing sales in the South of France, Spain and Germany meant that the company was renamed, Sunseeker International.

Throughout the following three years a new style of boat to complement Sunseeker's first high performance boats was developed. A range of boats sharing similar physical characteristics evolved. Angular shapes on the superstructure matched the high decks and steep-shinned hulls but was sympathetic to the performance qualities of the boats. As a result, the mood of the customers of the time was catered for and the development of the brand was enhanced as a Sunseeker could now be recognised at a glance. The company achieved another first at the time by producing the XPS 34. The design of this production boat, that married a pleasure boat with a racing hull, was an early example of what was to come to be known as 'High Performance Styling'. Indeed, this design became the first production boat to win the London to Calais offshore race and added the Round Britain Race title to her tally. Other firsts for the company included; the popular Rapallo 36; the Cobra 39 which was the first Sunseeker with triple diesels; and the Jamaican 35 which introduced Sunseeker's first Flybridge yacht.

At this time the boating industry as a whole had become so caught up in producing the boats it wanted to build, that little thought had been given to how the customers were

Above: *A new hull being lifted.*
Below: *One of Sunseeker's production facilities.*

actually using the boats. Once again the innovative Sunseeker recognised this problem and seized the opportunity to rectify it. The customers wanted large cockpits to take lots of people, required only occasional overnight accommodation and used their boats for enjoyment, fun and high performance. With this in mind the Portofino 31, a wide and comfortable two-cabin boat was designed and over 300 were sold. This confidence was consolidated with the launch of the Malibu 47, the first Sunseeker with tunnel drives, which enjoyed enormous success at the top of the luxury boating market.

During the late 1980s, whilst performance was never any less important, style became even more so. Sunseeker catered for this demand by taking note of what was happening in the car industry and introducing softer, less angular shapes in its designs. The Mustang 20 was Sunseeker's first example of this new style. This was followed by a number of other striking models including: the Tomahawk 37; the Mohawk 29; and the Thunderhawk 43. The Hawk 27 combined high performance with luxurious accommodation and intelligent, ergonomically considered features. The first Offshore Cruiser to adopt the curvaceous new styling was Sunseeker's, Camargue 46. This was a big family cruiser with an elegantly swept fore-deck, a stepped side deck and a curved windscreen backing onto a deep and lavishly fitted cockpit. The interior was equally lavish using materials not usually seen in British boatyards such as, birdseye maple contrasted with high gloss lacquer work and Alcantara trimming.

Above: *Renegade 60.*
Right: *A Sunseeker Predator 80 off Brownsea Island.*

It was partly due to these designs that Sunseeker International won the Queen's Award for Export Achievement in 1987. This feat was repeated in 1989 and 1994 making Sunseeker the only boating company to have been awarded the distinction three times!

Sunseeker had awakened a desire amongst its customers for even bigger boats and had to rely on its innovation once again in order to meet this demand. In 1990, the company came up with the Renegade 60, the first production cruiser ever to be powered by water jet propulsion. The Renegade combined performance with exceptional manoeuvrability and even the competition applauded when the first boat easily negotiated her way into a difficult berth at the Southampton Boat Show. Indeed, this model helped Sunseeker to establish its position as one of the leading boat builders in the world.

Robert's ambition did not stop there however, and in the following three years the expansion of the Sunseeker range continued. Models were introduced in all four ranges: Performance; High Performance; Flybridge; and Offshore Cruisers. Notably, among these new models was the Comanche 40 and the Predator 63. The Comanche had a jetski provided in a direct-entry garage beneath the aft sunbed and the Predator had a specially designed four metre, five seater. jet-driven, 35 knot ski-boat that could pop in and out of the stern for use as a tender or just for added fun!

In 1995 the Royal Yachting Association voted Sunseeker International, Boat Builder of the Year. Two years later, in order to maintain this high reputation an all new, purpose built shipyard was constructed on the Quay in Poole enabling the production of larger boats than ever before. The Superhawk 48 delivered a completely new level of high performance with a boat capable of speeds up to 60 knots but with a diesel engine that was also fuel efficient. In 1997 the marine industry was set alight with the launch of the world's largest production boat, the awesome Predator 80. The perception at the time, that large boats generally meant reduced performance offering vast accommodation but requiring a permanent crew, was shattered by the Predator 80. The Predator was an open-deck Performance Motoryacht that was also available as a hard-top option and her 50 tons could reach speeds in excess of 40 knots! Indeed, the success of the model was expanded when the Predator 58 and the Predator 54 were added to the range. Sunseeker achieved yet another milestone in its history in the same period with the launch of the Manhattan 80, the first production superyacht.

During the following three years the company launched a number of distinctive boats. The Portofino 34 was the first Offshore Cruiser to benefit from the company's new in-house lacquering facilities. The company also built the Superhawk 50, a boat of superyacht quality offering three-cabin accommodation and a 50 knot performance. However, the launch of the Apache 45, stylistically similar to the Superhawk but slimmer and sleeker, gave the company a valuable insight into customer perception. The design was too radical for the customer and at first did not sell well, although customers are now more ready to accept the evolution of the range. The company learned from this experience and the launch of the Manhattan 58 was extremely successful. This Flybridge yacht brought a new approach to interiors. At the time the interior of most production boats had a pronounced glitzy American feel with lots of chrome and peach decor. Sunseeker appointed the naval architect and stylist Ken Freivokh to design the interior of the Manhattan in an elegant style. Another hugely popular boat launched during the same period was the Offshore Cruiser, the Camargue 55. The performance of this model was revolutionary, aided by the introduction of a computerised engine management system.

The year 1992 was an auspicious one for Sunseeker's managing director, Robert Braithwaite. It was in this year that he was included on the Queen's Birthday Honours List making him, Robert Braithwaite MBE!

Above left: *Portofino 28.*
Top: *Malibu 47.*
Below: *The biggest ever Sunseeker, the 105 Yacht, to be launched in Autumn 2000.*

Towards the end of the 90s Sunseeker continued to make advances in styling, but one of the biggest influences over the design of the range was due to engine technology and the possibilities presented by advanced composite materials and new construction techniques. The company employed a team of talented young designers led by John Braithwaite in order to harness these new techniques. Indeed, during this time the Manhattan 44 was launched, as was the Manhattan 84 which was one of the biggest production and highly specified high-performance yachts in the world. The Predator 75 was added to the range of Performance Motoryachts and the Camargue 44 was added to the range of Offshore Cruisers. The Manhattan 64 and the Manhattan 56 completed Sunseeker's fleet of flybridge boats. Other boats added to the range at this time included: the Camargue 50; the Predator 68; and the Superhawk 40. With its fearless attitude to design evolution, Sunseeker then took High Performance craft to its extremes with the conception of the XS2000. This 38 foot sports/race boat was developed using a design by Fabio Buzzi, famous for his offshore racing and design successes.

The company has recently acquired the former Bolson's Shipyard which has a history in shipbuilding dating back to the 1930s. This maritime history is set to continue with further development and modernisation by the Sunseeker International Shipyard and will house the production of the new Sunseeker semi-custom 105 Yacht to be launched in the autumn of 2000.

The latest James Bond movie 'The World is Not Enough' features a Sunseeker in it's opening, pre-title sequence boat chase. Using a Sunseeker Superhawk 34, the scene is rumoured to be the longest and most expensive shoot for a single scene, ever in a James Bond movie. The boat's handling and manoeuvrability surpassed the film crew's high expectations and as a result the storyboards were adapted to make the stunts even more exciting. James

Bond is known worldwide for the best of everything one desires, ranging from gadgets, boats and cars and the company is excited to have been involved with such a prestigious project.

Today, Sunseeker International leads the globe in the development of large, fast, production motoryachts. The company has come a long way from its first year turnover of £129,358. However, the vision that it has always held, of striving to create the best possible motoryachts by employing whatever skills, techniques or materials are necessary, is still upheld today. This innovative approach will no doubt enable Sunseeker International to continue to make waves in the industry and around the world for many years to come!

Above: The Superyacht Shipyard.
Below: A Predator 80 at Sunseeker shipyard.

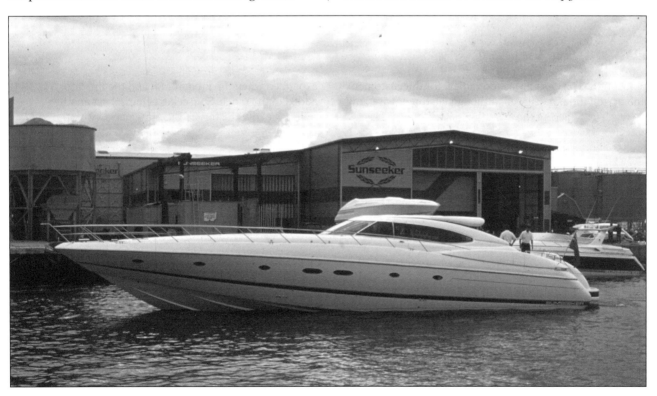

Fitting success for a family firm

Hawkes Shoe Shop was established in Poole in 1847, although there are indications that in fact the business was trading on a small scale from as early as 1808. It is still run by the Hawkes family, and this in itself makes the firm unique in Poole, as no other local business still trading today has stayed in the founder's family for this length of time. The founder of this firm, master bootmaker Joseph C Hawkes, was the son of a yeoman farmer from Longfleet. He spotted the potential of providing boots for the local fishermen who sailed from Poole harbour to fish cod on the banks of Newfoundland, and proceeded to make, by hand, leather thigh and knee fishing boots studded with brass plugs and guaranteed to give a lifetime's wear. The other kind of boot which Joseph Hawkes specialised in was the hand-made agricultural or navvy Derby, double-tongued and studded with hobnails.

Right: *A view of Hawkes shop taken in 1847.* **Below:** *Staff pose for the camera outside the shoe shop in 1913.*

All these boots were made in the front of the shop, and children and adults alike used to love watching Joseph Hawkes at work. First he would cut tops out of the cowhides and the greasy seaboot leather, using paper patterns. These pieces of leather were then sewn together; the boot was stitched inside out, so that when it was turned the right way out the seams would lie flat. Once the tops were completed,

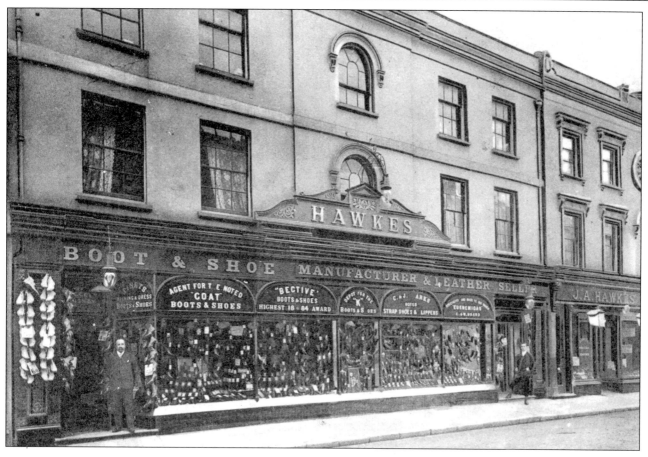

the welts and soles were attached with a 20-strand hemp thread well coated in tallow and beeswax; and when the sole had been stitched on, the whole boot was given a liberal coat of beeswax which soaked into the leather to make it waterproof.

For the ladies, Joseph Hawkes made elastic-sided walking boots in either horse skin or French calfskin. When these boots were finished, young boys were employed to polish them, applying blacking and spittle and rubbing it in with a deer-bone. This process took up to a day, but gradually the shine emerged, and eventually turned into a glassy jet-black patina, the likes of which we shall never see again.

By 1897 there were three Hawkes shops in Poole: one in the High Street, another in Ashley Road, Parkstone, and the third in Lower Parkstone. Later another branch was opened at the far end of the High Street at Longfleet. The original Poole shop was the largest shoe shop in the town, and was patronised by most of Dorset and Hampshire. Trade had become so brisk that it became necessary to bring in shoes from other makers, and Hawkes began to sell ready-mades from factories which are still household names today, such as K and Clark's.

Top: *Another view of the store in 1897.*
Left: *A window display featuring 'K Shoes' from the 1940s.*

This picture: *A discerning customer tries on a selection of shoes in a beautifully decorated children's shoe department which had a goldfish pond, a cage of budgerigars, a turtle and a rocking horse, all to keep the children amused whilst having their feet measured.*

The success of the business in the early 1900s led to the purchase of more shops, especially in the growing town of Bournemouth, where branches were opened in Westbourne Old Christchurch Road, Holdenhurst Road, Southbourne Grove and High Street Wimborne. Each shop had its own manager. The managers were people whose entire working lives were spent with the firm, from starting as school leavers right through to retirement. Those were the days, too, when shop workers worked long hours; shops would be open from eight o'clock in the morning to half past ten at night.

In the 1950s and 60s Hawkes' chain of shops continued to prosper - until the supermarkets moved into the main shopping areas. Initially it was the grocers and greengrocers whose trade suffered, but before very long the supermarkets began selling clothing and then footwear, beginning with Wellingtons and plimsolls, and moving on to fashion shoes. This was no help at all to the small independent shoe shop.

In response, Hawkes changed their selling profile, moving out of the fashion trade to concentrate on selling Clark's children's shoes. They became the main fitting agent for Poole, Bournemouth and the Dorset area, holding a guaranteed stock of over 10,000 pairs of children's shoes in all sizes and in fittings from B to H. Trade in

children's shoes boomed; even with up to 24 staff selling school shoes, it was not uncommon for customers to have to wait for up to half an hour to be served. Queues built up, stretching right out of the shop and up the road; and the sight of these queues obviously impressed other local entrepreneurs because soon five more shops appeared selling the same shoes at the same price, eager to share in Hawkes' success.

During the 1980s and 1990s trade declined, chiefly as a result of shoes being made to last longer. One by one Hawkes' branch shops closed down, and the shop in Poole High Street once again became the main outlet. This shop was fully refitted and modernised in 1997 to bring it right up to date, and at the same time the focus was switched to the other end of the age range when Hawkes ceased being a children's shoe fitter and specialised instead in fitting shoes for the over 45's.

Top: The changing face of the store, this time pictured in the 1950s. ***Above left:*** *A window display featuring Morlands boots, shoes and slippers.* ***Below:*** *Hawkes shoe shop in the 1990s.*

The right ingredients for success

To ascertain the origins of The Ryvita Company Limited, one has to go back well over 70 years in time to the home of Campbell Garrett. Campbell Garrett was a man dedicated to his trade and he had collected volumes of secret recipes for a multitude of different bread varieties. This specialist knowledge and expertise in the bread industry gave him a considerable advantage over his competitors.

After discovering crispbread and realising the commercial potential of this product, in 1925 Campbell Garrett and his family decided to import the product from Sweden into the United Kingdom and so, the first steps of what was to become The Ryvita Company Limited, were taken. After establishing the company in this way, the Campbell Garrett family were able to set up a local baking

Right: *Field Marshall Lord Montgomery opening the Ryvita Mill.* **Below:** *A typical production day in the factory during the 1960s.*

facility to support the burgeoning business. Birmingham was chosen as the base for this new company and 'Ryvita' was manufactured from this Birmingham site. Consequently, The Ryvita

Company Limited, accomplished two firsts in the industry. 'Ryvita' became the first crispbread makers in the United Kingdom and also became the producer of one of the first packaged goods in the bakery field.

The advent of the second world war brought with it several crucial changes for The Ryvita Company Limited. The Birmingham factory suffered considerable damage when it was hit by an early incendiary bomb. As a result the company was forced to move from the Birmingham factory and disperse throughout the country. Several smaller units were opened in Leicester, Edinburgh and York to compensate for this closure of the former base in Birmingham, during this time the Mill was still located in Birmingham.

Campbell Garrett decided to sell the business to Rowntrees in 1939. This ownership by Rowntrees was to last for the following ten years. A decade later however, in 1949, the company was sold on once again. Garfield Weston took ownership of Ryvita, soon to become part of Associated British Foods (ABF), and it was decided to centralise the operations once again.

Prior to Garfield Weston's acquisition of The Ryvita Company Limited in 1949, its baking facilities were geographically diverse. However, this changed in the same year that 'Ryvita' was purchased. Garfield Weston bought a new factory in order to consolidate production. The rye mill remained in Birmingham, where it was closer to the traditional rye growing areas of East Anglia. However, the new factory was located in Poole. Poole was chosen because of its port which enabled rye grain to be brought from Europe until the local farmers were able produce enough to cope with the demand. Indeed, today, 100 percent of the rye used on site is grown in the UK.

The year 1950 proved to be a year of distinction for The Ryvita Company Limited even reaching regal proportions! It was in this year that the company was issued with a Royal Warrant for 'Ryvita' and this could boast that the crispbread was eaten by the Queen!

From moving to their initial factory in Poole, The Ryvita Company Limited has continued to function from there, thus maintaining its strong connection with the area. The new mill was built in 1967 in order to form an integrated unit by providing milled rye for the bakery and it was opened in the April of 1968 by Field Marshall Lord Montgomery.

The 1960s were marked for the 'Ryvita' company by challenges from Europe. European manufacturers were trying to win the market from 'Ryvita'. Fortunately the company, rising to the challenge admirably, kept the European competitors at bay with their product quality and successful marketing techniques and in this way continued to move forward successfully.

The following decade saw The Ryvita Company Limited continuing to flourish. Indeed, the 1970s became memorable years for the business and its brand name.

The Ryvita Company Limited had produced only one type of crispbread since 1925. The year 1975 therefore, as well as being the 50th anniversary of 'Ryvita', was another landmark year in the history of the company. The 'Original' style crispbread for which the company was renowned was added to in

Below: Ryvita Mill (Poole) being built. It houses a rye mill, maize mill and wheat mill.

97

this year when the decision was made to broaden the range and diversify the product. The first addition to the range was a brown 'Swedish-style' product . The introduction of this product proved to be prosperous for the company as it helped to open further the export markets.

The 1980s were years of further expansion and product diversification for the company. In 1980 developments in extrusion cooking caused the introduction of new product concepts. The company's resulting extruded crispbread, 'Crackerbread' was launched and went on sale in this year. The following year, in 1981, a satellite production unit was opened in Stockport, Greater Manchester to cope with the extra demand for the new products. This unit was the company's second bakery.

The year 1983 saw the introduction of 'High Fibre' Crackerbread followed a year later, in 1984, by the 'Wholemeal' variant of crispbread. In the same year extrusion cooking techniques were exploited by the

company in order to diversify further and launch a range of breakfast cereals.

The 'Sesame' variety of crispbread was launched in 1987 and became extremely popular. Indeed, The Ryvita Company Limited is the largest user of sesame in the UK, even managing to out-do McDonalds! This was followed by Ryvita Multi-Grain in March 1996.

The latest product to be introduced is a sweet variety of Ryvita - Ryvita Currant Crunch, this was introduced in 1998.

Today, The Ryvita Company Limited continue to produce all of the product ranges developed throughout the 1980s and before. The factories are still equipped with state of the art baking equipment and run 24 hours a day, five days a week for 50 weeks of the year, employing over 400 people. The ingredients first used in 1925, including rye, water and salt, are basically the same today. Also, the company still remains the only manufacturer of crispbread in the United Kingdom. Its success is such that they hold more than a 90 percent share of the UK crispbread market, where 50 percent of households eat 'Ryvita'. This popularity is partly due to the fact that 'Ryvita' has secured a position in

*Above: Ryvita Currant Crunch is the latest addition to the Ryvita range. **Below:** A Ryvita lorry of the 1960s.*

Ryvita message changed from family values to exclusively women's appearance.

During the 60s well-known female icons such as Julie Andrews were used to further endorse the female benefits. The Ryvita message was encapsulated in the very successful and memorable 'Inch War Campaign', which carried right up until the 1990s.

Today Ryvita's advertising reflects the contemporary women. It is no longer diet related, it's now about health and versatility, epitomised by Ulrika Jonsson in the 1999 'Ulrika's Ryvita's' campaign.

'The Ryvita company Limited', although constantly expanding, nevertheless manages to maintain its original character as a local, family company. A total of three Westons have been involved in the company from running the bakery to managing the entire company! The company helps local schools with work experience and careers advice as well as supporting a variety of local fundraisers and helping to train managers within charities in business activities. As the company reaches its 75th anniversary in the year 2000 and looks to the future, one of its many ingredients of success - its 50 year connection with Poole, is set to continue.

which it is both a brand name and a product - whenever people think of crispbread they automatically think of 'Ryvita'! The company is also strong in exports. 'Ryvita' sells in over 87 countries from Alaska to Australia and, unusually for a food company, they have also achieved the Queen's Award for Exports, twice! Indeed, over 2.4 billion slices of 'Ryvita' are produced each year - enough to stretch for more than 150000 miles, or in other words, circle the world six times!

Ryvita Advertising

Advertising is an important part of Ryvita's heritage. One of Ryvita's strengths has been its long belief in the value of advertising and even more in the consistency of its message.

Early packaging was regarded as an advertisement in its own right, especially with no commercial television, magazines were also very strong and Ryvita used this medium to its full potential.

Advertisements in the 20s and 30s were placed in various publications such as Punch and the Daily Mail - the messages within these adverts were aimed at the family as a whole and health giving properties. In the 40s the message moved exclusively to the health benefits of Ryvita.

After the war, press advertising was placed in female fashion magazines of the day such as Vogue and the

Above: An aerial view of the Ryvita site.
Below: The latest Ryvita advertising campaign featuring Ulrika Jonsson.

More than a century of success built on firm foundations

The marriage of the Cornishman, Meichizedick James to his French fiancee in Guernsey in 1868 was to become a significant event in the history of estate agents, James & Sons. Following his marriage, Meichizedick James moved with his new wife to Poole in order to embark on their married life. The couple purchased from a stonemason for a sum of £190, No.60 Denmark Road, where he is described as a bookseller. In 1873 he set up in business as an estate agent and in 1888, moved to No.32 Poole Hill, Bournemouth.

In 1890 he was joined by his son, J B James and in 1899, Meichizedick ensured that the James name was once again to be seen in Poole, when they purchased premises at Ringwood Road. The firm's success continued and at the turn of the Century they purchased a third office at 117 Commercial Road, Parkstone.

Another Bournemouth office was added to the collection at Fishermans Walk Terrace, Stourwood. This expansion was exemplified when in 1908 M James & Son was advertised in the local press as being in Poole, Parkstone, Bournemouth and Stourwood.

Reginald Charles James, the second of Meichizedick's sons, joined what was now the family business adding to its expansion with more staff rather than offices! His timing was poor however and soon after he joined the company, came the advent of the first world war. Reginald was called up to serve in the forces and dutifully took temporary leave of the family business to serve his country. The war brought yet more changes to the estate agency and the Parkstone office changed its address from Commercial Road to Station Approach, whilst the office in Southbourne was closed, reducing the firm

to three branches. With the close of the first world war, James & Sons began to make progress once again. The Parkstone office premises were able to be re-purchased in 1923 for the sum of £950, despite having only been sold for £200! However, this turned out to be a solid investment and the premises remained in the family business until 1941. The inter-war years brought further development for the company and offices opened in Charminster and in 1924, 15 Branksome Terrace was purchased, now known as Poole Hill.

1928 saw yet another James generation joining the family business. Frank Courtenay James, a qualified surveyor and auctioneer, joined when his father retired after over three decades of service to the business. In 1937 yet another office was opened by the firm and this was to be the last expansion before the second world war. The advent of the second world war brought with it tragedy for the James family. Frank was looking after the business single handedly whilst his uncle Reginald was temporarily assisting the District Valuer. However, on the 10th January 1941, Frank was killed by enemy action whilst in the garden of his home in Canford Cliffs Road. Tragically, Frank's father also died during the war, leaving only Reginald to carry James & Sons forward.

Above: Melchizedick James, who founded the firm in 1873. Right: A brochure from the 1930s detailing some very desirable properties.

Unfortunately Reginald had to close two branches of the business as another negative result of the war, with only one office remaining at Poole Hill.

The end of the war brought a period of change to James & Sons. Two new Partners, Eric Dancy and Ellen Ruth Bond joined the company and in 1948 the firm opened a new office in Haven Road, Canford Cliffs. After over four decades of service, Reginald retired, handing the family business over to another new partner, William John Trim.

Under John Trim's guidance, the firm expanded further with offices in Moordown, Highcliffe, Wimborne, Fordingbridge and Blandford.

Various changes took place to the Partnership and in 1972 James & Sons acquired the Poole firm of

Belbens and in 1973 the Poole firm of Harker Curtis, thus re-establishing itself back in Poole town centre. After joining the firm in 1968, Roger Lees was promoted to Partner to run the Poole branches. Several further changes to the Partnership occurred during the 1980s, until 1987 when the Partners sold the firm to the Halifax Building Society, who ran the operation as part of Halifax Property Services.

In 1992, Roger Lees bought back the Commercial Department of the firm and re-established the company back in premises in Poole under the name of James & Sons. In 1993, Simon Walsham became a Partner, having been with the firm since 1985. James & Sons is now one of the leading firms of Chartered Surveyors in the area specialising in surveys and valuations, property management services and sales and lettings of commercial property.

The area covered is far and wide with properties managed in Bristol, Alton, Worthing and the Isle of Wight. The Partners now look forward to overseeing James & Sons into the 21st Century.

Top: *The firm's old Bournemouth Head Office.*
Left: *The current partners, Simon Walsham and Roger Lees.*

Making a splash in the heart of Poole

Over thirty years ago, in 1964, a new development in Poole began to take shape - an Arndale shopping centre which was to become The Dolphin Shopping Centre as it is known today.

The completion of the centre was the culmination of five years planning by Poole Council who wanted to make maximum use of the thirteen acres of land available to them in the centre of the town. In 1964 the Arndale Property Trust, which subsequently became part of Town and City Properties was appointed by the council to carry out the project following a scheme based on a layout prepared by Geoffrey Hopkinson, a Borough Architect and the Town Planning Officer. Looking at the Dolphin Shopping Centre today bustling with its many visitors enjoying their shopping experience you would not imagine the hours of intensive discussions that were held before the scheme was even approved. Eventually however, in 1965 the site was declared a Comprehensive Development Area and permission to go ahead with the development was granted by the smallest margin of only one council vote! Indeed, even the construction of the building became a challenge. The first half ton plate glass window shattered as it was lowered into place! These initial hiccups were soon overcome and a regional sports centre and central library were completed to compliment the new shopping centre.

When it opened in 1969, the fully covered, centrally heated and air conditioned Arndale Centre with its plantings, landscaping and seats was a new and different way of shopping. The residents of Poole could now enjoy a pleasurable shopping "experience" in the warmth and comfort of the centre. The covered walkway from the shopping centre through the High Street of Poole leading to the bus, railway stations and the multi-

storey carpark, added convenience and easy access to the list of advantages for the centre's first shoppers. The Arndale Centre proved to be hugely popular and in 1970 the success of this new and different shopping experience even attracted a delegation from St Brieuc in Brittany to discover what Poole had achieved.

The achievements did not stop there. The success of the site meant that the second stage of the Arndale Shopping Centre could be undertaken as early as 1980. This involved extending the site to incorporate other major tenants. The popularity of the centre was such that even crows nesting on the huge crane used in the construction wanted to be part of the action. These unwanted tenants eventually flew the nest and made way for other, more popular ones, such as: Marks &

Top right: The Mayor of Poole opening the Arndale Centre in 1969.
Right: An early view of the main concourse.

surveyor, died of cancer aged only 26 and so to commemorate her life a plaque was erected at the foot of the panoramic lift installed during the refurbishment.

The new name of the centre - Dolphin, was chosen to compliment its new look. The name also reflects the centre's unique historical location with Poole's finest beaches only five miles away and the fishing port and quay only one mile away. Indeed, Poole's coat of arms incorporates a dolphin and local legend has it that dolphins used to be spotted in Poole Bay. A plaque commemorating the official opening of the centre can be found on the upper floor. Other more extensive improvements include lifts, elevators, superb facilities for the disabled, an attractive water feature and more diffuse lighting and plantings which help to create a contemporary atmosphere.

Today, the Dolphin Centre continues to bring the Poole community together and receives over 157 000 visitors a week, with numbers rising considerably over the busy Christmas period which is an important time for the centre. Every year Father Christmas arrives in Poole on a R.N.L.I. lifeboat and then makes his way to his grotto at the Dolphin via a parade through the town. Naturally, in

Spencer, Beales Department Store, C&A, Boots, Littlewoods and more than 100 others which are still to be found in the centre today.

1989 saw the emergence of the Dolphin Centre as it is known today and the end of the old Arndale Centre. A major 8 million pound re-furbishment was undertaken to lead the shopping centre into the 21st Century. Erdman Lewis Ltd became the new managing agents running the centre as part of their 30-strong portfolio of centres nationwide on behalf of PosTel Property Services. Tragically, one of PosTel's employees, Angela Conroy a chartered investment

honour of this special visitor the Dolphin is seasonally decorated and appearances from the stars of the local pantomime add to the festive atmosphere. Throughout the year fundraisers, exhibitions, promotions, roadshows and celebrity appearances capture the imagination of the visitors and enhance their shopping experience. Indeed, the Dolphin Centre is still Dorset's premier shopping venue and with plans for a massive millennium party in February 2000, it is set to continue making a splash in Poole!

Top: *Children enjoying the Arndale Centre in the mid 1970s.* ***Above:*** *The Dolphin Shopping Centre in 1999.*

A group of young clowns aboard a decorated cart are ready to take part in the annual Poole Carnival.

Acknowledgments

We are grateful to Mr Andrew Hawkes for his permission to reproduce the photographs of S W Batting as well as postcards from the 'Poole Collection of Andrew Hawkes'.

Thanks are also due to
Peggy Burns for penning the editorial text
and Ann Ramsdale for her copywriting skills.